Redefining the Terms
of Trade Policymaking

by Susan Ariel Aaronson

Foreword

by Senator Max Baucus (D-MT)
Chairman, Senate Finance Committee

I n 2000, Congress and the administration worked successfully together on trade policy. Our accomplishments included passage of the China Permanent Normal Trade Relations bill granting China PNTR status once the World Trade Organization (WTO) accession procedures are completed, a monumental achievement; passage of legislation on trade with Africa and an enhanced Caribbean Basin Initiative (CBI) program; congressionally approved changes in the Foreign Sales Corporation in response to a decision at the WTO; and passage of a Miscellaneous Tariffs Act. The U.S.-Jordan Free Trade Agreement and the U.S.-Vietnam Bilateral Trade Agreement were negotiated and signed by the Clinton administration and, as of early June, seem to be moving forward. This diversity of agreements reflects the importance of trade.

Expanding trade in goods and services is necessary to drive the U.S. domestic economy as well as the global economy. A top priority of the United States in 2001 and beyond is to continue to make progress on trade liberalization and opening markets around the world. But trade liberalization must be done in the proper way.

To make further progress on trade liberalization and opening markets, we must first rebuild the consensus on trade in this country. This must be a top priority for Congress and the administration. It will require a political consensus, which means a public consensus, demonstrating to all citizens that trade and expanding markets contribute to their prosperity and to a better quality of life; addressing legitimate labor and environmental concerns in trade agreements; enforcing U.S. trade laws and using them aggressively; and fundamentally fixing the Trade Adjustment Assistance program so that the United States can provide real training and assistance to displaced workers.

Rebuilding the consensus on trade will take time. The administration will have to work closely with Democrats and Republicans in Congress to ensure that we have the proper environment in which to make further progress on trade. The Clinton administration tried twice in recent years to secure fast track—with no success. I must stress that there will be no consensus unless we can figure out how to deal with legitimate labor and environmental concerns in fast track legislation.

There are a number of explanations for the eroding consensus on trade. First, many Americans believe that the benefits of globalization are inequitably distributed. Even if they benefit from globalization, they still feel that the benefits are fragile. This sense of fragility has been heightened in recent months by the stock market decline, by indicators of slowing economic growth, and by fear of a recession.

Second, the increasingly atomistic nature of our national legislative process has contributed to the loss of a consensus on trade. The day when a small group of congressional leaders made most key decisions is over. But we need effective management of the congressional process. Twenty years ago, only a handful of congressional offices had a staff member with trade expertise. Now, almost every Senator and House member has at least one legislative assistant who follows trade issues closely, and many members of Congress are themselves true trade experts. This is good. But we have not made adjustments in the way that Congress works to facilitate taking these discrete points of expertise and transforming them, or aggregating them, into a more coherent whole.

Third, issues such as labor rights and the environment need to be accommodated before we can make much more progress on trade liberalization. So how do we rebuild this consensus on trade? Let me suggest four areas to pursue.

First, we must address the legitimate concerns regarding labor rights and the environment. This means making an honest effort to address the relevant issues at the intersection of trade and labor rights and the intersection of trade and the environment. Presidents cannot muscle an old-fashioned, "clean" fast track bill through Congress. This is a new era, and everyone needs to work together to create a middle ground on these issues. I am not suggesting that we can address all environmental and labor concerns in a trade agreement. However, we should be able to incorporate some key labor and environmental issues in trade negotiations. After all, we have environment and labor side agreements as part of the North American Free Trade Agreement. The recent U.S. textile agreement with Cambodia includes labor rights provisions. GSP, CBI, and the Africa bill all involve labor rights provisions. As we do this, we should work under the principle that "one size does not fit all." Different countries and different negotiating contexts require different solutions. The second area in rebuilding the consensus on trade is to enforce America's trade laws. In any society, failure to enforce its laws and rules leads to a debasement in the functioning of that society. Similarly, in the international trading system, failure to enforce trade laws leads to a proliferation of the worst, most unfair, and damaging practices. We must also work harder to ensure full compliance with new agreements, as well as compliance with the hundreds of bilateral, regional, and multilateral agreements we already have. We need to do a much better job of monitoring trade agreements. When our trading partners fail to comply with an agreement, it corrupts the negotiating process and leads to a loss of confidence in the trading system. My proposal to create a Congressional Trade Office is one way to help do this (see Chapter 4).

The third area is to provide meaningful worker adjustment programs. Our system of trade adjustment assistance has failed. The financing is insufficient. The programs often train workers for non-existent jobs. The scope of the programs is too narrow; we should figure out a way to deal with adjustment on farms.

The final area in rebuilding the consensus on trade is to ensure that citizens feel that they are part of the process. This means that we in Congress, as the elected representatives, must participate much more actively in trade policy. Congress does not and cannot negotiate trade agreements. We do not implement trade agreements, and we do not enforce them. But Congress can and should set the policy direction for the country, establish trade priorities, and exert oversight on how the executive branch is implementing trade policy and trade laws. We have not done a good job of this in recent years, and that must change. Congress is a vitally important instrument in ensuring that the public sees what the executive branch is doing. Congress provides the critical vehicle for citizens to feel that they genuinely have access to the trade policy process. Another way to make citizens feel that they are participating is to improve the trade advisory process. It must become more inclusive. It must become more open. The trade advisory process is a creation of Congress, and Congress needs to fix it.

We are at a critical juncture in trade policy. For 50 years the United States has led the way to open markets and trade liberalization. The United States took the lead in building the world trading system. But this was possible only because there was a political consensus in favor of trade liberalization. If we are serious about leading the struggle for open markets, we must start by rebuilding that shattered consensus.

The series of seminars conceived and organized by Susan Aaronson made a major intellectual contribution to rebuilding the consensus. The sessions provided an opportunity for all sides to discuss their views in a calm setting. Policymakers need more of this type of informed dialogue.

Foreword

by Congressman Amo Houghton (R-NY)
Member, House Ways and Means Committee

I s it a new dawn for trade policy? Perhaps. Certainly with about 95 percent of the world's population outside the United States, it is not an area to be ignored. To do so will be at our own peril. There are many trade issues on the horizon, both at home and abroad.

First, we need a more united front regarding trade policy. It should not be a political matter—it is a jobs issue. Depending on the circumstances, imports may or may not create jobs. Exports absolutely create jobs. We should not get all tied up in the process. We need a clear eye, whether it be with fast track (now called trade promotion authority), foreign sales corporations, which is both a trade and a tax issue, or enforcement of U.S. trade laws. U.S. markets are open. Trade agreements just have to open foreign markets and reduce trade barriers.

Congress and the administration need to find a bipartisan path through the "trade forest." The goal should be the same. Due to the lack of fast track for the past few years, many believe that the United States has fallen behind in finalizing bilateral trade agreements. A number of agreements are in various stages of negotiation, and these should be aggressively pursued to completion.

In terms of the other groups that affect trade policymaking, we need to look at the policies of the World Trade Organization, the International Monetary Fund, and the World Bank to see if they are working in concert on trade-related finance issues. Where possible, we should make recommendations for greater coherence.

Last, we should do much more to foster public understanding of U.S. trade policy. After all, the bottom line is how trade policy affects individuals. We need to put a human face on trade. That brings us back to jobs. We must better communicate the importance of international trade to jobs in this country. We cannot ignore overseas markets. South America, for example, is a huge market, and the Free Trade Area of the Americas initiative needs to be pursued immediately. Opening up the South American markets by lowering or eliminating tariffs would be beneficial to all. But we must communicate that benefit.

Susan Aaronson put together a timely seminar series on trade policymaking. Whether we agree on all the trade issues is not the test. The test is to work together to arrive at a trade policy that benefits the working people of the United States.

Acknowledgments

T his book would not have been possible without the input, advice, and good ideas of Paul Magnusson, *BusinessWeek*; Libby Bingham, Executive Director, Washington International Trade Association, who helped to organize the trade seminars; Valerie Ploumpis, European-American Business Council, for providing excellent feedback on my ideas; Ambassador Anthony Quainton, President and Chief Executive Officer of NPA, who let me vent many of the ideas of this book; Martha Lee Benz, for her skillful editing; Mary A. Haldeman, who expertly processed the many drafts; James Reeves, who is a wonderful colleague; and the other members of NPA's staff. The book was inspired by the scholarship of I.M. Destler of the University of Maryland.

I alone am responsible for the recommendations in this book. *The sponsors and the speakers who are listed below were not asked to endorse these new ideas; rather, they supported the process of developing them.* The views expressed also do not necessarily represent those of NPA.

This book is dedicated to my husband, Doug Wham.

SPONSORS OF NPA'S TRADE SEMINAR SERIES

I want to express great appreciation to the following organizations for their support of the seminar series:

AOL
Archer Daniels Midland Company
The Boeing Company
Bunge Corporation
Cargill, Incorporated
Communications Workers of America
Daimler Chrysler Corporation
Enron
The Financial Times
Food and Allied Services Trade Department, AFL-CIO
Friends of the Earth
GPC International
Institute for Agriculture and Trade Policy

Intel Corporation
League of Women Voters
Louis Dreyfus Corporation
Mitsubishi Motors
National Wildlife Federation
New York Life
Procter & Gamble Manufacturing Company
Toyota Motors North America
United Food and Commercial Workers International Union
United Steelworkers of America
Verizon Communications
Viacom, Inc.
Washington International Trade Association

SPEAKERS AT THE SEMINARS

I would also like to thank the following seminar speakers:

Mark A. Anderson, President, Food and Allied Services Trades
Department, AFL-CIO

Bertus Van Barlingen, Director, Trade Section, European
Commission

Jagdish Bhagwati, Arthur Lehman Professor of Economics and
Professor of Political Science, Columbia University, and
André Meyer Senior Fellow, International Economics,
Council on Foreign Relations

Eric Biel, General Counsel, Fontheim International

Brian Bieron, former Policy Director, House Rules Committee, and
Vice President, Clark & Weinstock

Phyllis O. Bonanno, former Assistant USTR Public Liason, and
President, CrossStreetTrade, Inc.

Jake Caldwell, Trade and Environment Program Manager,
National Wildlife Federation

Robert C. Cassidy, Jr., Partner, Wilmer, Cutler & Pickering

Steve Clemons, Executive Vice President, New America Foundation

I.M. Destler, Professor and Director of the Center for International and Security Studies at Maryland (CISSM), University of Maryland

Tim Hodges, Economic Counselor, Canadian Embassy

Jon E. Huenemann, former Assistant USTR for North American Affairs and Vice President, GPC International

Robert Kuttner, Editor, *The American Prospect*, and Columnist, *BusinessWeek*

Laura Lane, Director, International Public Policy, AOL

William C. Lane, Vice President, Government Relations, Caterpillar Inc.

Nancy Leamond, former Chief of Staff to USTR Charlene Barshefsky

Paul Magnusson, Washington Correspondent, *BusinessWeek*, and moderator of NPA's trade seminars

Mark Ritchie, President, Institute for Agriculture and Trade Policy

Bruce Stokes, Senior Fellow, Council on Foreign Relations

David Waskow, International Policy Analyst, International Program, Friends of the Earth

David Witzel, Founding Partner, Forum One

Ira Wolf, Senior Advisor on Trade Policy to Senator Max Baucus (D-MT)

About the Author

S usan Ariel Aaronson is Senior Fellow for International Programs at the National Policy Association. She is the author of *Taking Trade to the Streets: The Lost History of Public Efforts to Shape Globalization; Trade and the American Dream: A Social History of Postwar Trade Policy; Are There Trade-Offs When Americans Trade?;* and *Trade Is Everybody's Business.* Aaronson received her Ph.D. in economic history from Johns Hopkins University and has taught at the University of North Texas, George Washington University, and George Mason University. She has also been a Guest Scholar in Economics at the Brookings Institution.

Introduction

T o America's 43rd president, George W. Bush, trade and freedom are directly linked. In his view, "free trade brings greater political and personal freedom." Moreover, "when we ship goods and products that improve the lives of millions of people," America is exporting freedom. Thus, using trade agreements to "free" trade is an important component of the president's international and domestic agenda.[1] His trade priorities include participating in the Free Trade Agreement of the Americas, which would liberalize trade among the 34 nations of the hemisphere, as well as a new round of global trade talks under the aegis of the World Trade Organization (WTO).

But the president is not free to pursue this agenda without the consent of Congress. This shared responsibility for trade was delineated in the Constitution by America's founding fathers. They gave the president responsibility for managing foreign affairs, while Congress was "to regulate commerce with foreign nations" and to "lay and collect . . . duties." This shared authority made sense because, by definition, the executive tended toward internationalism, including economic internationalism, whereas Congress was more receptive to local and often more protectionist concerns.[2]

While it has not always been easy to share authority, the executive and Congress developed an effective trade policymaking partnership in the 20th century. In 1934, Congress passed the Reciprocal Trade Agreements Act, which radically altered the trade policymaking process by changing the procedures and the players. Congress granted the president limited authority to negotiate bilateral trade liberalization, if bilateral trade agreements could be shown to create jobs. But the president could reduce only tariffs and not other forms of trade barriers, and he could grant tariff concessions only if they did not injure U.S. producers.[3] Furthermore, Congress passed the Trade Act of 1974, which granted the president authority to negotiate nontariff trade barriers (NTBs) such as subsidies and procurement regulations as well as traditional barriers to trade (border measures such as tariffs). In a series of procedures that became known as fast track, the act provided for strict congressional monitoring of the scope of negotiations and spelled out a process for adjusting U.S. law if necessary. For some 20 years, these fast track procedures enabled the president and Congress to negotiate and approve historic bilateral and multilateral trade agreements, including the U.S.-Israel, U.S.-Canada, and North American Free Trade Agreements, as well as the Tokyo and Uruguay Rounds of the General Agreement on Tariffs and Trade (GATT), the precursor organization to the WTO.

However, Congress has not granted new fast track authority to the executive since 1993. In addition, Congress, the concerned public, and the administration disagree not only about the objectives of trade policy, but also about the scope of trade agreements. The United States has moved forward on bilateral trade agreements, as well as on new agreements provided under the 1993 authority. But Congress has not provided the assurance that it will approve without amendment a trade agreement the president negotiates. That assurance is embedded within fast track. Without congressional/executive agreement on the future of trade policy, the United States will surrender its traditional leadership role in trade liberalization.

A growing number of interest groups from America's left and right have banded together to oppose both the fast track process (which many view as undemocratic) and the actual content of trade agreements (which many view as undermining other important policy goals such as protecting the environment or promoting human rights). These trade agreement critics include the AFL-CIO, environmental groups such as the Sierra Club, and activist groups from the left (Greenpeace) and the right (Phyllis Schafly's Eagle Forum).[4]

Most Americans, however, were not cognizant of this debate until the Seattle ministerial in December 1999, the first time that the United States had hosted a ministerial meeting to launch a new round of global trade talks. Some 30,000 protestors from around the world took to the streets to criticize trade agreements. The protests became front page news. Reporters struggled to describe who the trade agreement critics were and why so many had taken to the streets.

Most trade liberalization advocates were dismayed by the protests and unsure what to do about them. President William J. Clinton said that he shared the protesters' concerns about the WTO's lack of transparency and that he would continue to work to make the world trading system more equitable.[5] The Director General of the WTO, Michael Moore, described the ministerial as a "disappointment."[6] *The Financial Times* characterized it as a "disaster" and a "wake-up call."[7] The ministerial certainly woke up the American public, who came to understand that trade policy was important to their daily lives. *However, policy differences are not the only factor that bedevils progress on trade policy.* To some degree, progress is hampered by the institutional structure within which trade policy is made. Many agencies are involved in making trade policy and monitoring trade agreements. In 2000, the General Accounting Office (GAO) examined the implementation and enforcement of trade agreements and declared that no one knows exactly how many trade agreements America is a signatory to. GAO also stressed that no one agency or cabinet official is in charge of trade policy.

The responsibility for trade is shared by the Departments of Agriculture, Commerce, State, and Labor, the Environmental Protection Agency (EPA), and other agencies, as well as the U.S. Trade Representative (USTR), an executive branch agency. USTR is the lead agency, with the responsibility to develop, administer, and monitor more than 400 trade agreements. Considering the size and scope of these agreements, USTR is both understaffed and overburdened. Given the importance of trade to the U.S. gross domestic product (trade accounted for almost one-third of GDP in 2000), it is appropriate to review the institutional structure of trade policymaking, promotion, and monitoring.

Despite the importance of trade to the health of the American economy, trade policy is not built on a foundation of public support and understanding. Polling data from the 1940s to the present reveal that although the public is supportive of trade agreements, it fears that trade agreements can undermine American norms and sovereignty.[8] This attitude should signal to policymakers that they need to make a different, albeit more comprehensive, argument for trade agreements as tools to govern globalization. Proponents of trade agreements should let the record of freer trade policies speak in a comparison of jobs lost and gained, of benefits and costs to unskilled as well as skilled workers, of benefits and costs to American (and global) health and environmental standards, and of the effects on democracy.

OUTLINE OF THE BOOK

This book examines how Americans might help foster a new consensus on trade by thinking differently about the way that the

United States makes trade policy. Designed to help policymakers improve trade policymaking, the book reflects issues discussed at a series of trade seminars sponsored by the National Policy Association in Washington, D.C., from October 2000 to March 2001. Each chapter presents specific problems, background information, analysis, and recommendations. A final chapter by Paul Magnusson provides an overview of the trade seminar series.

The seminars were an unusual approach to building dialogue. They were sponsored by 17 corporations, 4 unions, and 5 civil society groups. (See the "Acknowledgments," pages xi–xiii, for the list of sponsors.) These groups have widely differing views on trade, but they share a belief that trade policymaking has become too contentious. *It is important to note that the sponsors did not necessarily endorse or oppose the recommendations; rather, they supported the process of trying to develop new ideas.* The audience, which included members of the Washington policymaking, academic, business, civil society, labor, and diplomatic communities, provided fresh perspectives and challenged many ideas.

NOTES

1. Testimony of Robert B. Zoellick, U.S. Trade Representative, before the Committee on Ways and Means, U.S. House, March 7, 2001, p. 1, at www.ustr.gov.

2. John M. Dobson, *Two Centuries of Tariffs: The Background and Emergence of the United States International Trade Commission* (Washington, DC: Government Printing Office [GPO], 1976), pp. 8-9, 31.

3. Susan Ariel Aaronson, *Taking Trade to the Streets: The Lost History of Public Efforts to Shape Globalization* (Ann Arbor: University of Michigan Press, 2001), pp. 50-51.

4. On the GATT, see Susan Ariel Aaronson, *Trade and the American Dream: A Social History of Postwar Trade Policy* (Lexington: University Press of Kentucky, 1996), pp. 147-166. On NAFTA, see John J. Audley, *Green Politics and Global Trade: NAFTA and the Future of Environmental Politics* (Washington, DC: Georgetown University Press, 1997), pp. 155-163. On Schafly, see www.eagleforum.org/column, February 29, 1996, and October 31, 1996. For more recent examples of criticism from the left, see www.wtowatch.org, and from the right, Alan Tonelson at the U.S. Business and Industrial Council at www.usbic.org.

5. Excerpts from the press conference by President Clinton, December 8, 1999, and from the press briefing by Joe Lockhart, December 6, 1999, can both be found on the WTO Third Ministerial Conference Web site, www.wto.org.

6. The statement by Michael Moore can be found at www.wto.org/wto/new/press160.htm.

7. Editorial,"WTO: Disaster in Seattle," and Guy de Jonquieres and Frances Williams, "Seattle: A Goal Beyond Reach," in *Financial Times*, December 6, 1999.

8. Aaronson, *Trade and the American Dream*, polls cited on pp. 99-100, 168-174.

1

What Should the Turf of Trade Agreements Be?

THE PROBLEM

rade agreements regulate how firms can trade and how policy-makers can protect producers and consumers from injurious imports. Until 1979, trade agreements governed the use of tradition-al commercial policies—tariffs and quotas. But policymakers gradu-ally recognized that, with or without intent, some regulations and policies distorted trade between foreign and domestic producers. In the Tokyo Round of the GATT, policymakers approved rules to control the use of nontariff barriers such as subsidies and consumer regulations.

Policymakers continued to expand the purview of trade agree-ments in the 1980s and 1990s. In the Uruguay Round, government officials approved rules governing the trade distortion of food safety and intellectual property regulations. By 2000, the WTO included more than 142 member nations that adhered to its rules on trade in services and goods. Many nations were also eager to sign bilateral and regional trade agreements.

By the 1990s, bilateral and multilateral trade agreements had become one of America's main policy tools to regulate some of the most complicated issues of globalization, from public health to environmental protection. Moreover, because these agreements provided enormous leverage with countries that desired stable trade relations with the United States, many policymakers and citizens wanted to use the agreements to achieve a wide range of nontrade policy goals. The goals included promoting economic growth in Mexico and rewarding Jordan for its approach to peace in the Middle East. At the same time, however, some citizens in the United States and other nations began to question the growing scope of trade agreements; they believed that the agreements elevated the promotion of trade objectives above the achievement of other equally important policy goals.

Policymakers are at a fork in the road. They must decide whether trade agreements should be revamped to facilitate other vital policy goals or if trade agreements should govern trade alone. If trade agreements continue to include rules covering the potential trade distortions of social or environmental regulations, they may undermine support for trade liberalization.

BACKGROUND

Although America is blessed with navigable rivers, fertile soil, abundant resources, a hard working populace, and a huge internal market, the United States needs to trade because it cannot efficiently or sufficiently produce all the goods and services that its citizens require. Further, there are some goods that America cannot produce. Thus, from its first days of nationhood, the United States has signed trade agreements and treaties of commerce with other nations.

Just as political leaders do today, America's founding fathers frequently disagreed about the objective and scope of trade policy—what might be called the "terms" of trade policy. For example, most of the men who sat down to write the Constitution believed that they must make protection of human rights a top priority. After all, they had just fought a war to obtain their rights as citizens. At the same time, plantation owners in the South, which had been devastated by the Revolutionary War, insisted that they needed slaves to rebuild the southern economy. Most delegates agreed with Roger Sherman of Connecticut that "It was better to let the southern states import slaves than to part with those states."[1] The founding fathers therefore decided that preservation of the union was more important than the human rights of slaves.

Ultimately, delegates from the South pointed their way to a compromise. Article I, Section 9 of the Constitution did not prohibit the migration or importation of slaves prior to 1808. But it allowed the states to impose a tax or duty on trade in slaves, not to exceed $10 for each person.[2] This compromise promoted unity, economic development, and trade between the states.

However, the compromise did not remedy the conflict between America's trade policy and its human rights policy. Moreover, the compromise affected the trade policies of many of the new nation's important trading partners. Before the Civil War, the North and the South had achieved a tenuous middle ground that limited the expansion of slavery. America's northern and western economies were indirectly dependent on the product of slave labor. Great Britain and other manufacturing nations also indirectly benefited from slave labor because British and European mills finished products using American cotton, grown, picked, and packed by American slaves. The troubled relationship between America's trade and human rights policies was not resolved until the Civil War. Congress abolished slavery in 1865. The United States gradually began to improve its human rights record. It was among the first nations to ban goods manufactured by forced (prison) labor through the Tariff Act of 1890 (Section 51).[3] The architects of the GATT included a similar provision, and it was subsumed in the WTO.

Human rights have not been the only nontrade issue to intersect and impact the development of trade agreements. In 1910, for example, Congress made it unlawful to manufacture, import, export, or ship any misbranded or adulterated insecticide. The United States, Russia, Japan, and Great Britain signed the Fur Seal Treaty in 1911, which regulated the hunting and importation of seals.[4] The Federal Seed Act of 1912 prohibited imports of adulterated grains and seeds.

So policymakers have long struggled with the problem of attempting to expand trade agreements while not thwarting the achievement of other important policy goals. Sometimes they made nontrade objectives squarely part of a trade agreement (or treaty) such as the Fur Seal Treaty. Sometimes they designed trade agreements to accommodate both trade and other public policy goals such as advancing human rights abroad. Nevertheless, during the first 30 years of the GATT, from 1948 to 1978, the relationship between trade policy and human rights, labor rights, consumer protection, and the environment was essentially "off-stage." The GATT's role was limited to governing how nations used traditional tools of protection, border measures such as tariffs and quotas. The United States, the world's largest market and the main driver of the GATT, set those limits.

The GATT

The GATT was tailored to fit the legislative authority granted to the executive under the 1945 extension of the Reciprocal Trade Agreements Act. Congress allowed the executive to negotiate commercial policies only.[5] Thus, the GATT said almost nothing about the effects of trade (whether trade degrades the environment or injures workers) or the conditions of trade (whether disparate systems of national regulation, such as consumer, environmental, or labor standards, allow fair competition). However, Article XX of the GATT permitted nations to restrict trade when necessary to protect human, animal, or plant life or health or to conserve human resources. Such exceptions could not be arbitrary or a disguised restriction on international trade. Nonetheless, throughout this period the United States consistently pushed for the inclusion of fair labor standards in the GATT. For example, Nixon administration officials decided that labor standards must be part of the GATT, but they maintained that trade negotiators "must make absolutely clear that we do not intend to make labor standards a subterfuge for protectionism."[6] Their efforts did not succeed. Although the preamble of the GATT recognized the link between trade and employment, the GATT was never expanded to include labor standards.

The GATT also said little about domestic norms or regulations. In 1971, the GATT established a working party on environmental measures and international trade, but the group did not meet until 1991, after much pressure from some European nations.[7] During those years, few policymakers would admit that their systems of regulation sometimes distorted trade. Such regulations were the turf of domestic policymakers, not foreign policymakers or trade negotiators.[8] Nevertheless, domestic policymakers, including members of Congress, still wanted to protect certain sectors such as textiles and watchmaking. Because the GATT limited their ability to use traditional protectionist tools, policymakers became more creative in developing other mechanisms to protect, such as voluntary restraint agreements, quota arrangements, and procurement regulations. Policymakers also realized that social and economic regulations gave domestic producers a slight market advantage over their foreign competitors; domestic firms found it easier to comply with the regulations and to amortize their costs.

However, as these more creative nontariff trade barriers began to proliferate, U.S. trade policymakers, economists, and business leaders began to worry. They understood that domestic regulations, such as health and safety regulations, could distort trade with or without intent.[9] They worked to include rules governing the use of regulations such as trade barriers within the GATT and other trade agreements. This process began in the Tokyo Round (1974-79) and was completed during the Uruguay Round (1986-93). Policymakers expanded the turf of trade agreements to include rules on domestic policies covering intellectual property, food safety, and subsidies, among others. In addition, they created a new international organization to subsume the GATT, the World Trade Organization.[10]

It is ironic that the effort to develop global rules to govern global trade has created a backlash against trade agreements. A growing number of citizens believe that the United States has subordinated control over its social and environmental regulations by including them within trade agreements. To prevent trade agreements from undermining such regulations, these critics have divided into two camps. One camp argues that trade agreements should be a floor for harmonizing regulations and wants to improve trade agreements; the other camp believes that America's high regulatory standards can best be protected by excluding social and environmental issues from trade agreements.

Dissonance on trade is as old as the nation and as American as apple pie. Nevertheless, such disagreement is undermining support for trade agreements and for economic internationalism in general. Moreover, dissonance in trade is undermining U.S. credibility because America does not speak with a consistent voice on how best to reconcile the desire to promote both trade and the objective of raising social and environmental standards.

SOLUTIONS

As members of the Business Roundtable, an organization of chief executive officers from America's largest, most prestigious companies, recently noted, "We must first build a national consensus on trade policy. . . . Building this consensus will . . . require the careful consideration of international labor and environmental issues . . . that cannot be ignored." The Roundtable concluded that the problem is not whether these issues are trade policy concerns. Rather, the problem is that trade proponents and critics must find a strategy, a trade policy approach, that allows negotiators to address these issues constructively.[11]

Ambassador Robert B. Zoellick, the current U.S. Trade Representative, has signaled his willingness to seek ways to accommodate social and environmental objectives with trade expansion goals. However, he has not signaled how he will do so—whether within trade agreements, through side agreements, through mechanisms being used by other countries, or with policies that complement trade objectives. For example, foreign aid can be used to help developing countries improve their ability to create and enforce national laws protecting the environment and human and labor rights. Trade agreements can be linked to an internationally accepted code of conduct (as the Canadians proposed for the Free Trade Agreement of the Americas). Another strategy might be to help corporations and civil society improve living and environmental standards. An example of such an approach is the Ethical Trading Initiative (ETI), an ongoing collaboration between the British government and industry, nongovernmental organizations (NGOs), and trade unions. ETI's goals are "to develop and encourage the use of a widely endorsed set of standards embodied in codes of conduct and monitoring and auditing methods which will enable companies to work together with other organisations outside the corporate sector to improve labour conditions around the world." The ETI is working to create tools for developing best practice in the field of ethical trading as well as monitoring systems for those tools.[12] It is a key part of British trade policy and is certainly worthy of U.S. review.

To find common ground on future trade policies, citizens and policymakers must first develop a common language about what trade agreements do. Americans need to start talking about trade agreements as one of several tools that can be used to govern the global economy. This approach will produce greater public understanding of what the United States does when it negotiates trade agreements and why such agreements are necessary. It is an approach that will also encourage a more honest debate about trade.

There is no one model for trade agreements, given the diversity of goods and services as well as the political and economic differences among America's many trading partners. Moreover, trade agreements, by definition, are amendable. Trade agreements have evolved to include rules on a wide range of policies, from border measures to subsidies. They have also evolved to address social and environmental goals. NAFTA was the first trade agreement to formally link trade policies to environmental and social policy goals by including those issues in side agreements. The U.S.-Jordan Free Trade Agreement, in contrast, took a different approach by calling on each nation to establish and enforce its own labor and environmental laws and not to make changes that may distort trade.

Nor is trade policy the only or best policy tool to govern globalization. Trade agreements have much to commend them. Countries want to sign trade agreements with the United States because it is a huge and wealthy market. U.S. policymakers recognize that agreements give them leverage to induce America's trading partners to make policy changes in other key arenas from intellectual property to human rights protection. But the use of that leverage may not be the most effective way to encourage policy changes in other countries. Trade agreements by themselves cannot end poverty, reduce disease, protect the environment, or convince corrupt policymakers to respect human rights. To achieve these goals, foreign aid, channeled through international and nongovernmental organizations, may be a more appropriate mechanism.

Trade policy is most effective when it is targeted at what it does best—expanding imports and exports and limiting how and when policymakers can protect American producers and consumers. At the same time, policymakers must find ways to ensure that trade agreements do not undermine other crucial policy goals. Policymakers should put equal energy into creating alternative strategies. These could include making foreign aid more effective, developing global policies and rules to conserve the global commons, and creating incentives to help corporations maintain high standards in their overseas operations as well as in the operations of their suppliers and subcontractors.

RECOMMENDATIONS

- There is no one model for trade agreements. Policymakers should develop different approaches to or models for trade agreements that accommodate different objectives, trading partners, and government policies.
- Policymakers should limit their reliance on trade agreements to achieve nontrade goals. At the same time, they should work hard to ensure that trade agreements promote, rather than undermine, the achievement of other important policy goals such as conserving the environment, preserving peace, and promoting human rights. The United States should attempt to develop strategies such as the Ethical Trading Initiative to achieve these diverse and equally important goals.

NOTES

1. W.E.B DuBois, *The Suppression of the African Slave-Trade to the United States of America, 1638-1870* (New York: Dover Books, 1979), pp. 2-3, fn. 2.

2. Ibid., pp. 53-62.

3. Susan Ariel Aaronson, *Taking Trade to the Streets: The Lost History of Public Efforts to Shape Globalization* (Ann Arbor: University of Michigan Press, 2001), p. 44.

4. Percy Bidwell, *The Invisible Tariff: A Study of the Control of Imports into the United States* (New York: Council on Foreign Relations, 1939), pp. 105-107, 111-115.

5. U.S. Tariff Commission, *Operation of the Trade Agreements Program*, 2nd report (Washington, DC: GPO, 1949), pp. 3, 12, 19-21.

6. Aaronson, *Taking Trade to the Streets*, p. 54, fns.110-113.

7. Steve Charnovitz, "Environmental and Labour Standards in Trade," *World Economy* 15(3)(May 1992), pp. 338-339.

8. Ibid., pp. 341, 348.

9. Margaret E. Keck and Kathryn Sikkink, *Activists Beyond Borders: Advocacy Networks in International Politics* (Ithaca, NY: Cornell University Press, 1998), pp. 41-47; and Bidwell, *The Invisible Tariff*, pp. 106-107, 109-111.

10. GATT Secretariat, "Final Act Embodying the Results of the Uruguay Round of Multilateral Trade Negotiations," December 15, 1993, Annex IV, p. 91.

11. Business Roundtable, "The Case for U.S. Trade Leadership: The United States Is Falling Behind," statement on February 9, 2001, p. 16, available at www.brt.org.

12. See www.ethicaltrade.org/html/aboutfaq/content.shtml.

2

Strategies for the Executive Branch and Congress to Share Trade Authority

THE PROBLEM

T | he United States is unique in that the legislature and the executive share responsibility for trade policymaking under the Constitution. Thus, trade policymaking by design is a tug of war between the two branches. For much of American history, Congress was in the driver's seat. However, after the passage of the Reciprocal Trade Agreements Act in 1934, Congress reluctantly ceded some of its control over trade policymaking to the executive. From 1934 to 1974, Congress kept the executive on a short leash, forcing the executive to follow procedures for public input and to return to Congress for new authority. Those procedures, however, did not build public support for trade agreements nor quiet congressional criticism that executive leadership of trade policy was undemocratic.

Congress struggled to find a new balance that would allow it to retake control of trade policymaking while permitting the executive to complete existing negotiations and to bring new sectors under the aegis of the GATT/WTO. Fast track was the result. Fast track can be defined as a series of legislative procedures set forth in the Trade Act of 1974. These procedures stipulate that once the president formally submits to Congress a bill implementing an agreement (negotiated under the act's authority) concerning nontariff barriers to trade, both Houses must vote on the bill within 90 days without amendment.[1]

Policymakers need to weigh key questions about how to modernize the trade policymaking process. First, is fast track necessary? Fast track may not be the only or best way for the president and Congress to share authority. Although fast track is a congressional innovation, fast track appears undemocratic to some observers. Trade proponents defend fast track by arguing that it is essential—they presume that America's trading partners will not negotiate without fast track. Yet the Clinton administration negotiated several important trade agreements without such authority from Congress. USTR Charlene Barshefsky often argued in her last year in office that she did not need fast track to begin a new multilateral round of trade talks.[2] The cur-

15

rent USTR, Ambassador Robert B. Zoellick, disagrees. He has made attainment of fast track, which he renamed "trade promotion authority," a key priority.[3]

Second, is there a more effective way for Congress and the executive to make trade policy in an open, transparent, flexible, and timely manner?

BACKGROUND

The Trade Act of 1974 was a radical change in U.S. trade policymaking: it created fast track to further the ability of the president to negotiate NTBs under the GATT. This was the first time Congress acknowledged that domestic regulations and subsidies, among other policies, might distort trade and that it might be necessary for the legislature to change those policies in the interest of facilitating trade. The act also set up a system of advisory committees designed to make trade policymaking more democratic and transparent (see Chapter 5). The act was historic for other reasons as well. In the Jackson-Vanik amendment, Congress explicitly linked trade policy to Soviet willingness to improve its human rights record. By so doing, Congress set a precedent: it made social and environmental results acceptable objectives for some trade agreements. Congress also made it easier for groups not directly concerned with the economic effects of trade, such as environmentalists, to influence trade policies.

Tough Times

Congress was motivated to make these changes because of difficult domestic economic and political conditions. Legislators were under significant pressure from influential business constituents to attack barriers to trade, especially NTBs. The NTBs included a wide range of subsidies, procurement regulations, and product standards. As Chapter 1 pointed out, it was evident by the 1960s that policymakers in the United States and abroad were increasingly creative in using these barriers both to regulate and occasionally to protect. However, the GATT did not include rules governing NTBs.[4]

The United States was also bedeviled by stagflation in the 1970s. Policymakers recognized that imports might keep prices down. They hoped that trade liberalization would also expand demand for U.S. products. In 1973, the Organization of Petroleum Exporting Countries' oil embargo and rising oil prices led to massive layoffs in the automobile industry and then affected other sectors. Companies found it hard to adjust to higher energy prices. Mounting food and petroleum prices led to a collapse in demand, eventually resulting in recession and unemployment.[5] In such tough economic times, President Richard M. Nixon needed a foreign policy success. He wanted a trade agreement with the Soviet Union to increase exports and cement his program of détente. But his timing was poor. He submitted a trade bill at the same time that the public learned of the Watergate scandal. Congress responded by carefully scrutinizing his request. Nixon's proposals also came at a frightening time in the world. On October 6, 1973, the Yom Kippur war erupted. Some members of the House argued that if Nixon sought to change the paradigm for foreign policy to détente, they wanted to change the model for making trade policy to give Congress greater control over agreements that the executive proposed and negotiated.

The House hearings on the president's bill were rancorous and focused on whether Congress should grant the president authority to negotiate NTBs. The president's men made their case in conciliatory tones, recognizing that their request raised questions of constitutionality. According to Ambassador William R. Pearce, Deputy Special Representative for Trade Negotiations, "We can't ask you for an advance grant of authority to do away with NTBs; in most cases, they are linked in very subtle ways to all sorts of domestic legislation."[6] The president's request also raised the issue of federalism. Congressman Peter Frelinghuysen (R-NJ) expressed grave worries about negotiations on NTBs that were "so inextricably intertwined in a web of domestic social, economic, and political considerations that Congress would benefit by knowing what the executive branch had in mind before it entered into negotiations."[7]

The Road to the Trade Act of 1974

The 1974 debate presaged many of the concerns expressed about GATT and NAFTA in the 1980s and 1990s. Congress was particularly interested in how granting such authority might affect health and safety standards at the federal, state, and local levels. Congressman James C. Corman (D-CA) questioned whether Oregon's law prohibiting the importation of beverages in nonreturnable containers could be negotiated away by the president.

Congressman Charles A. Vanik (D-OH) asked the General Accounting Office how a grant of that authority might affect environmental protection laws such as those protecting endangered species. The GAO replied, "A President may not through trade negotiations overturn or change a duly enacted law, absent other authority of law. However . . . the President feels—and we agree—that the [bill] . . . will grant him sufficient authority to allow him to enter into agreements which could, in effect, change domestic law."[8]

Many of the witnesses and House members during the 1974 debate suggested that trade policies would be improved if trade policymaking became more democratic by involving a broader cross section of Americans. The Emergency Committee for Foreign Trade, a leading business lobby supportive of trade liberalization, urged that "the president consider the views of the public" on NTBs because the president must seek public comment before the executive enters into tariff negotiations.[9]

Despite days of debate, the House never acted on the president's bill. The Senate delayed consideration of that bill and ultimately invented a new approach—fast track—for congressional approval. This approach requires Congress to vote to authorize negotiations and later to approve the negotiations. Fast track resolutions also include a set of formal negotiating objectives.[10] Congress explicitly designed these changes so that it would have access to more information and greater flexibility in making decisions about the ever-broader turf of trade negotiations. The changes were also designed to limit congressional interference in the negotiations.

The Senate debate did not focus on NTBs, but rather on the use of trade sanctions and market access to promote American values overseas. Congress was willing to expand trade with the Soviet Union and communist China, but only if they exhibited respect for human rights and permitted relatively freer emigration. The Ford administration found a compromise that linked trade concessions to human rights improvements. However, policymakers and witnesses during the Senate debate recognized that linking trade liberalization to the achievement of social goals in other nations might open up a Pandora's box of requests. As an example, the Society for Animal Protective Legislation wanted the bill to be amended to require Soviet adherence to an additional moratorium of 10 years on the commercial killing of whales to get normal trade privileges (then called most favored nation privileges).[11] Although those requests did not win congressional backing, they presaged the debate that would impact fast track in the years to come. How could trade and social and environmental policies be reconciled in bilateral and multilateral agreements that were designed to promote trade by reducing barriers to trade? Moreover, could the United States use the carrot of market access to change other nation's domestic policies? Was this an appropriate use of trade policy?

The Trade Act of 1974 was finally signed into law on January 3, 1975. The act was a first step in making trade policymaking more transparent, democratic, and accountable. By linking trade concessions to emigration, the act explicitly made the promotion of human rights an acceptable goal of trade policy. Moreover, by so doing, Congress acknowledged that trade policies could affect the achievement of other important policy goals and that some U.S. laws might have to be changed to ensure that they did not distort trade.

The Controversies Surrounding Fast Track

In recognition that NTB negotiations could affect U.S. laws and regulations—the turf of Congress—Congress outlined specific procedures for reviewing and approving trade agreements. An NTB trade agreement cannot "enter into force unless the president submits an authorizing bill for negotiations and an implementing bill."[12]

The authorizing bill should specify trade negotiating objectives and the type of agreement to which the authority applies (such as bilateral or multilateral). It should also set procedural recommendations for outside and congressional advisors. The implementing bill must contain the following provisions:

1. approval of the trade agreement;
2. changes or additions to domestic law necessary to implement the agreement; and
3. a statement describing changes to administrative practice (regulations) necessary to implement the agreement.

Congress, by majority vote, has 90 days to vote up or down on the bill after its introduction (the implementing bill may not be amended by Congress). If the bill is a nonrevenue bill, i.e., it does not propose changes to tariff schedules and the revenue they provide, the law specifies that Congress has only 60 days to vote up or down.[13] The floor debate in each chamber must be kept to 20 hours, a limitation designed to prevent Congress from getting bogged down on micro-issues or unrelated issues. However, some members, in particular Republicans, have used these provisions to "limit the inclusion of labor and environmental provisions not directly related to trade."[14]

The attempt to place such limitations may facilitate timeliness. But it has led some trade agreement critics to argue that the fast track process is flawed and undemocratic. Public Citizen, a Nader-affiliated watchdog group, argues that "No other such severe limitations of congressional authority exist in U.S. law. . . . Fast track . . . procedures force Congress into accepting hard compromises made in one area of negotiation needed to make gains in others." Yet that is the essence of how trade agreements are approved—the citizenry permits changes to protections affecting specific sectors to achieve the larger interest of reducing barriers to trade. Public Citizen also charges that fast track "allows many matters unrelated to trade to be 'superglued' onto trade legislation. Because no amendments are allowed, Congress is thus forced into rejecting trade agreements or approving special deals and unsavory arrangements."[15] But critics of trade agreements such as Public Citizen cannot have it both ways. On the one hand, they argue that environmental/consumer and human rights issues are related to trade. To facilitate review, those issues must be "super-glued." On the other hand, critics recognize that through fast track, Congress authorizes congressional participation in the negotiation. This process should ensure that Congress is aware of all "special deals and unsavory arrangements."

From 1975 to 1993, fast track promoted the sharing of power between Congress and the executive. In 1993, Congress granted an extension through April 15, 1994, to the Clinton administration to complete the Uruguay Round of multilateral trade talks, which created the WTO. Congress participated in and approved both the Tokyo and Uruguay Rounds. Congress also approved NAFTA and other bilateral trade agreements. But this system of power-sharing broke down around 1993-94, and President Clinton failed to gain new fast track authority in 1997 and 1998.

Pundits, scholars, and even congressional members disagree as to why President Clinton did not get congressional authorization to negotiate new trade agreements such as the Free Trade Agreement of the Americas. Some critics argue that fast track failed because it does not explicitly link labor and environmental protections to trade policy. Others argue that fast track is undemocratic because Congress does not have enough time to fully assess the impact of a trade negotiation on America and Americans. But, as pointed out, it is illogical to argue that fast track is undemocratic because it was invented by Congress. Nevertheless, fast track can be made more transparent for an Internet-age polity, as Chapter 5 discusses.

This author believes that no president has obtained fast track since 1994 because Congress has been again attempting to reengineer the balance between it and the executive on trade policymaking. Presidents can no longer claim a Cold War rationale for clinging to foreign policy powers granted to the executive. Furthermore, members of Congress recognize the increased importance of trade to their constituents; not surprisingly, they want more control over policies that affect Americans where they live, work, shop, worship, and learn.[16]

Yet it is precisely because trade policies have become so important that the executive and Congress must find common ground on strategies to reconcile trade and other important policy goals. Regardless of whether trade agreements should include other objectives, it is clear that Congress authorized such a link when it developed fast track through the Trade Act of 1974. Moreover, the Omnibus Trade and Competitiveness Act of 1988, the last major trade legislation that Congress passed, declared that promoting respect for worker rights was a principal negotiating objective of U.S. trade policy.[17]

From 1998 to 2000, few administration or congressional leaders sought to end the impasse over fast track. Members of the WTO were still digesting the Uruguay Round and arguing over its implications. The Seattle ministerial seemed to turn off many Americans and members of Congress from the politics of trade. American business did not appear to be hungry for major trade liberalization or another fight after the vote on whether China should obtain Permanent Normal Trade Relations from the United States. But as economic conditions began to deteriorate in the United States in late 2000, agricultural and business groups began to call for a renewed effort to gain fast track authority. They understood that they must deal with social issues. Business groups such as the Business Roundtable and the National Association of Manufacturers also sought to identify ways to address labor/environment issues within trade agreements, and in particular fast track. In separate efforts, both groups proposed a range of options to address social and environmental issues. These included helping to raise environmental and labor standards through foreign aid to developing countries, clarifying the relationship between the WTO and multilateral environmental organizations, and stressing that no single model applies to all trade agreements. Some Hill Republicans openly criticized these efforts. One anonymous Hill staffer complained that "Business may be getting too far out front."[18]

As noted, Ambassador Zoellick has made fast track a key priority in President Bush's ambitious trade agenda at the bilateral, regional, and multilateral levels. Zoellick changed the term fast track to trade promotion authority because fast track has an unpalatable connotation to some critics of America's approach to trade policymaking.[19] But a new name does not ensure a successful partnership between the two branches of government. The president and Congress must find new strategies for sharing the authority to create trade policy.

SOLUTIONS

The framers of the Constitution wanted trade policymaking to be a tug of war, with the branches jousting over control of such important public policies. Today, for the executive and Congress to effect a new approach to sharing the power to make trade policy, each branch must reassert its expertise and responsibilities.

Because Congress is responsible for regulating foreign commerce, it should take the lead in trade policymaking by annually specifying its priorities and objectives for trade negotiations. Congress should also hold yearly reviews of agreements negotiated by the executive. These reviews should assess how well the administration is meeting the congressionally determined objectives for trade. This process would return Congress to the driver's seat in trade policymaking. Further, as elaborated in Chapter 1, such reviews would bring a more honest debate about whether the United States uses trade policy to achieve too many objectives and whether other, more tailored policy tools could be better designed to meet environmental and social policy goals.

Congress should consider a tradeoff of strategy (fast track/trade promotion authority) for structure. It should grant permanent authority to the executive to negotiate trade agreements, as the noted trade scholar I.M. Destler has suggested, which would give the administration flexibility. Because the executive is responsible for foreign policy, it should not be hamstrung by Congress when the administration needs to move quickly to meet market conditions.[20]

In return for the granting of permanent authority by Congress, the executive should support the creation of a Congressional Trade Office (CTO). Congress needs a new structure such as a CTO to make trade policy. As Chapters 3 and 4 discuss, the CTO would review trade agreements, monitor implementation, and serve as a clearinghouse for public opinion. The CTO would be a counterweight as well as a complement to USTR, thereby returning to the shared authority between the executive and Congress envisioned by the framers of the Constitution.

Given the complexity of trade agreements, 90 days may be too short a time frame for congressional review of agreements. While the time of review should be limited, 120 days may be more appropriate. If an agreement is worthwhile, it should receive a full review. Moreover, this time frame would in no way alienate trade partners eager to sign an agreement with the United States.

Through the use of the strategies outlined here, Congress and the executive branch can more effectively share the power to make trade policy in an open, transparent, flexible, and timely way.

RECOMMENDATIONS

- Congress should take the lead in trade policymaking by yearly reviewing its priorities for trade negotiations, the objectives of such negotiations, and the administration's achievement of Congress's goals.
- Congress and the executive should develop a new approach to trade policymaking in which changes in strategy (fast track/trade promotion authority) are traded for changes in structure. Congress should grant permanent authority to the executive to negotiate trade agreements. In return, the executive should support the creation of a Congressional Trade Office.
- While Congress must adhere to a strict timetable for its review of trade agreements, 90 days is too short; 120 days may be more appropriate.

NOTES

1. I.M. Destler, *American Trade Politics*, 3rd ed. (Washington, DC: Institute for International Economics [IIE], 1995), p. 312.

2. Without fast track, Ambassador Barshefsky negotiated several agreements, including the telecommunications agreement, the financial services agreement, and free trade agreements with Jordan. She also obtained congressional approval of normal trade relations for China, a new Caribbean Basin Initiative bill, and the Africa Growth and Opportunity Act. Ambassador Charlene Barshefsky, "Thoughts at Moment of Transition," speech at the Economic Strategy Institute, December 19, 2000, p. 3.

3. On his desire for fast track, see the testimony of USTR Robert B. Zoellick before the Committee on Ways and Means, U.S. House, March 7, 2001, p. 3, at www.ustr.gov.

4. Susan Ariel Aaronson, *Taking Trade to the Streets: The Lost History of Public Efforts to Shape Globalization* (Ann Arbor: University of Michigan Press), pp. 60-65.

5. Allen J. Matusow, *Nixon's Economy: Booms, Busts, Dollars and Votes* (Lawrence: University of Kansas, 1998), pp. 219, 221.

6. Committee on Ways and Means, *Hearings on H.R. 6767, The Trade Reform Act of 1973*, 93rd Cong., 1st sess., part 1, May 9-June 15, 1973, pp. 352-353; Ambassador Pearce's comments, p. 395. Also see summary of government officials' comments on the basic authority, pp. 5175-5176. Administration officials were well aware of the congressional implications of negotiating NTBs. See W.B. Kelly, Jr., May 9, 1969, pp. 3-10, in D-4/69, Box 5, in Record Group 364, boxes of the State Department in the National Archives.

7. Committee on Ways and Means, *Hearings on H.R. 6767*, pp. 327-331, 5176-5177.

8. Ibid., pp. 557-558, 756-759, 763.

9. The League of Women Voters also urged that the interests of consumers be given serious consideration when national trade policy is discussed; ibid., pp. 370, 461, 2997, 5305; comments of Robert B. Schwenger (a former trade negotiator), pp. 4468-4489; V.J. Adduci, President, Electronic Industries Association, p. 3268; and National Council of Jewish Women, Inc., p. 2954. For a good summary of opinions of witnesses, see pp. 5177-5193. On attitudes toward NTB negotiations, see pp. 5193-5204. For the views of the Emergency Committee on Foreign Trade, see pp. 660, 668.

10. Committee on Ways and Means, *Brief Summary of H.R. 10710, "Trade Reform Act of 1973," Report to the House on October 10, 1973* (Washington, DC: GPO, 1973), p. 55; and Committee on Finance, *U.S. Senate Hearings on H.R. 10710: An Act to Promote Development of an Open Nondiscriminatory and Fair World Economic System* (Washington, DC: GPO, 1974).

11. Committee on Finance, *U.S. Senate Hearings on H.R. 10710,* p. 2585; link of MFN to environment, pp. 2649-2659.

12. Michael J. Glennon, Thomas M. Franck, and Robert C. Cassidy, Jr., *United States Foreign Relations Law: Documents and Sources, International Economic Regulation,* Vol. 4 (London: Oceana, 1984), pp. 40-45.

13. Ibid.; and I.M. Destler, *Renewing Fast-Track Legislation* (Washington, DC: IIE, 1998), p. 8.

14. I.M. Destler, "Fast Track: Options for the Process," in *Restarting Fast Track,* ed. Jeffrey J. Schott (Washington, DC: IIE, 1998), pp. 50-51.

15. Public Citizen, "Backgrounder: Fast-Track," at www.tradewatch.org/FastTrack/fast.html.

16. Susan Ariel Aaronson, "The Story Behind Fast Track," *Journal of Commerce,* September 11, 1997.

17. Section 1101(b)14 of the Omnibus Trade and Competitiveness Act of 1988. See Committee on Ways and Means, *Overview and Compilation of U.S. Trade Statutes* (Washington, DC: Ways and Means Committee Print, 1997), p. 853.

18. "Business Effort on Environment, Labor Link to Trade Hits Snag," *Inside U.S. Trade,* February 9, 2001.

19. See the testimony of USTR Zoellick before the Committee on Ways and Means, U.S. House, March 7, 2001, at www.ustr.gov.

20. I.M. Destler, "The Need for Fast-Track Authority," testimony before the Subcommittee on Trade, Committee on Ways and Means, September 30, 1997, at www.iie.com/papers/destler0997.htm.

3

New Institutional Structures
for Trade Policymaking

THE PROBLEM

A s trade has become more complex as well as more important to the health of the American economy, both Congress and the executive branch have struggled to manage trade policymaking. The Office of the U.S. Trade Representative, a small executive branch agency, is charged with developing, articulating, negotiating, and monitoring trade policies. To succeed at these many tasks, USTR must work effectively with Congress, as well as coordinate the disparate views of departments and agencies such as Agriculture, Commerce, and the Environmental Protection Agency (EPA) that also deal with trade. Congress too is involved in trade policymaking. However, Congress is not well organized to develop, monitor, and assess 21st century trade initiatives, which often overlap the committee structures. Meanwhile, some new organizations, such as the Clinton-developed coordinative arm, the National Economic Council (NEC), have challenged USTR's control of trade policymaking. Is there a more effective way to organize both branches of government to make, monitor, articulate, and enforce trade policies?

BACKGROUND

As discussed in Chapter 2, policymakers have long argued not only over the scope of trade policy, but also over which branch of government and agency should control it. The U.S. ability to negotiate bilateral and multilateral trade agreements is rooted in the Reciprocal Trade Agreements Act of 1934. That law allows the president to negotiate tariff concessions in trade agreements in return for equivalent concessions by other nations "only after exhaustive study shows that they will not result in material injury to any group of American producers."[1]

With the 1934 act, Congress ceded some of its control over trade policy to the executive branch. But the legislative branch remained in the driver's seat in making trade policy. The act kept the executive on a tight leash, forcing the president to return to Congress to obtain

27

renewed authority as well as feedback on the agreements that the
executive made. The law was designed to ensure that the Department
of State—an agency whose main mission was foreign policy—would
be responsive to the needs of specific sectors and would balance
"export promotion with import protection."[2]

From 1934 to 1962, the Department of State negotiated trade
agreements, developed trade legislation and policies, and solicited
public opinion. State also coordinated an interagency working group
to develop trade policy. However, because State Department officials
were not elected, some opponents of trade agreements argued that
agreements negotiated by State were undemocratic. Moreover, many
on Capitol Hill distrusted State, fearing that the department did not
effectively balance U.S. producers' and consumers' interests and
international interests. In response to those concerns, Congress created a new nonpartisan Office of the Special Trade Representative in
1962. The aim was to ensure that foreign policy objectives did not
trump other policy goals. President John F. Kennedy placed the
Special Trade Representative within the White House. The small staff
did its job well, coordinating between agencies as well as working
with them on negotiating the Kennedy Round.[3]

Challenges to the Trade Representative

There were challenges to the Special Trade Representative's control
over trade policy. In 1969, Commerce Secretary Maurice Stans tried
to take control of trade policy. In 1971, President Nixon established
a Council for International Economic Policy that attempted to subsume the Office of the Special Trade Representative. But in 1973,
Congress decided that the Special Trade Representative's status
should be enhanced. The Trade Act of 1974 created a new presidential office and gave cabinet rank to the Special Trade Representative.
Under this structure, the United States successfully participated in the
Tokyo Round of the GATT. However, several key senators, including
William Roth (R-DE), were still concerned that this organization was
not achieving what they deemed the proper mix of freer trade and
protection. Roth pushed for a Department of Trade that would subsume the Special Trade Representative's negotiating and coordinating
functions as well as the trade enforcement and monitoring functions
of other agencies such as Commerce and Treasury.

Recognizing that the office was losing ground, President Jimmy Carter gave it new and broader responsibilities and renamed it the Office of the United States Trade Representative. The office was assigned "international trade policy development, coordination, and negotiation functions." But the Department of Commerce was given control over subsidies and dumping cases, and the Department of Agriculture retained its responsibility for farm trade issues.[4] Thus, other agencies continued to play significant roles in trade policymaking, and leaders of those agencies would challenge USTR's control.

Moreover, this reorganization did not increase USTR's clout with members of Congress. Some officials continued to complain about USTR and to dispute the organization of trade policymaking between the branches of government and among agencies. In the 1980s, trade became more contentious. Key American industries such as steel and autos lost market share and demanded protection. In a bid for greater control over trade policymaking, President Ronald Reagan's Secretary of Commerce, Malcolm Baldrige, tried to revive the idea of a Department of International Trade and Industry, based on Senator Roth's proposal. But this proposal did not progress on Capitol Hill.[5] USTR continued as the lead in trade matters, while Commerce played a secondary role.

During this period, Congress reasserted its desire to gain greater control of trade policymaking. It forced the Reagan and George H. Bush administrations to adopt new strategies for pressuring major trading partners to open their markets. (Examples were the use of competitiveness policies and aggressive unilateral measures such as Super 301. Super 301 required USTR to designate several of America's trading partners as "priority foreign countries" because of their trade barriers and called for retaliatory protectionism if those countries did not reduce barriers. The strategy was thus termed "aggressive unilateralism.") Congress directed USTR to use the threat of protectionism to spur market opening policies among key U.S. trading partners such as Korea, Brazil, and particularly Japan.[6]

Reestablishing USTR's Leadership

However, President Bush's USTR, Carla Hills, used those tools to reestablish USTR's central role in trade policymaking.[7] She consistently took a tough stance on foreign protectionism and worked hard to negotiate both NAFTA and a new multilateral trade round. Her strategy promoted greater respect and support on Capitol Hill for trade liberalization. But NAFTA brought a different debate about trade policy. The issues were no longer only about jobs, sovereignty, or democracy. Nevertheless, USTR responded to traditional protectionist interests and did not anticipate, understand, or effectively respond to the new critics of trade agreements. Those critics, who came from human rights, environmental, development, food safety, and other backgrounds, did not have a direct economic stake in trade policymaking. But because they perceived that trade agreements were undermining other important public policy goals, they had a direct political stake. The USTR in the Bush administration was relatively insulated against the new politics of trade, but Hill's successor, Mickey Kantor, could not ignore such interests. The new players and politics came to have an important impact on the structure of trade policymaking.

As President Clinton's first Trade Representative, Kantor maintained USTR's leadership role in making trade policy. He successfully found a balance between the U.S.'s trading partners and the many competing interests in the Uruguay Round of the GATT. Both NAFTA and the Uruguay Round received significant votes of support from Capitol Hill.[8] Meanwhile, Kantor, and later USTR Charlene Barshefsky, built up the staff at USTR, adding personnel with expertise on the environment and food safety. In 1996, USTR created an office dedicated to monitoring and enforcing trade agreements. USTR also enhanced and broadened the advisory committee structure, including new players such as state and local officials (see Chapter 5 for further discussion).[9] As a result, USTR was better positioned both to anticipate public concerns about the substance of trade policymaking and to ensure that trade agreements were monitored, enforced, and, perhaps most important, litigated at the NAFTA and the WTO levels.

Meanwhile, as outlined in Chapter 2, Congress began to reassert its control over trade policy. After 1994, the Clinton administration was unable to convince Congress to grant it new authority to negotiate trade agreements such as expansion of NAFTA to Chile or creation of a Free Trade Agreement of the Americas. Congress made it clear that its voice must be heard on trade.

USTR also had to wrestle with a new organization in the White House, the National Economic Council, designed to coordinate economic policy among government agencies. According to I.M. Destler's extensive study of the NEC, the council "undermined" USTR's ability to coordinate trade policymaking. However, the NEC played less of a role in the second Clinton administration. Thus far, the George W. Bush administration has made it clear that it will not rely on a NEC-type organization in the White House to coordinate economic policy, although the administration has enhanced the role of the National Security Advisor in trade policymaking.[10]

Who Monitors and Enforces Trade Agreements?

The problem of organization is not just a question of who is in charge of making trade policy. The United States has negotiated so many trade agreements that some analysts have questioned whether it can benefit from them if it cannot monitor their implementation.[11] Because of this problem, Congressman William R. Archer, Jr. (R-TX, now retired), then Chair of the House Ways and Means Committee, asked the U.S. General Accounting Office in 1999 to examine the government's capacity to monitor and enforce its numerous trade agreements. GAO's study, issued in 2000, found that at least 17 federal agencies are charged with monitoring and enforcing agreements. According to the study, the agreements cover a broad range of issues from intellectual property to food safety. Monitoring means that the agencies must undertake complex tasks such as identifying compliance problems, analyzing information about them, and seeking ways to resolve them. GAO noted that this load will continue to grow.[12] The study stressed that the staffs at USTR, Commerce, and Agriculture are overwhelmed by monitoring and enforcement responsibilities. GAO concluded that the government is unable to maximize the intended benefits of its trade agreements because it cannot completely fulfill its monitoring and enforcement responsibilities.[13]

In fiscal year 2001, USTR received significant additional funds for its many tasks. But neither adding money or personnel can solve the issue of whether the United States is well organized to make, monitor, articulate, and enforce trade policies. President George W. Bush had his doubts. During the deliberations about who should be USTR, the president's transition team made public a debate about whether USTR should retain its cabinet rank. Reporters noted that Bush wanted Commerce Secretary Don Evans to take the lead on trade. Then Chairman of the Senate Finance Committee, Charles E. Grassley

(R-IO), and the ranking Democrat, Max Baucus (MT), insisted that USTR remain a cabinet-level position. Georgetown University law professor Dan Tarullo, who coordinated Clinton administration trade policy on the NEC, noted that it would be illogical for USTR to negotiate agreements while the Commerce secretary set overall trade policy. That step would tell the world that "the United States really doesn't think trade issues rise to the importance of cabinet-level discussion."[14]

SOLUTIONS

Given the importance of trade and the complexity of trade agreements, it is ironic that the president even considered downgrading the role of the U.S. Trade Representative. Because trade can affect the achievement of many other policy goals, its status should be enhanced. The president should propose to Congress that USTR be designated a cabinet agency, equal to the State Department and other executive branch agencies, and renamed the Department of Trade.

At the same time, the new Department of Trade should not subsume the trade functions of Commerce, Agriculture, EPA, or other departments. These departments bring valuable insights and constituents to the development of trade policy. Instead, the Department of Trade should coordinate these diverse views. This approach would elevate trade to the policymaking importance it deserves within the administration and maintain the needed diversity of views.

Some members of Congress claim they lack the staff expertise to make and monitor trade policy. Senator Baucus, now Chairman of the Senate Finance Committee, has called for greater congressional staff to deal with trade policymaking through a new, centralized Congressional Trade Office (see Chapter 4 for his recommendations). While almost all members of the committees that deal with trade, from Ways and Means to Agriculture, have a personal staff assistant who closely follows trade, members on other committees also need staff well versed in trade.

The CTO would make Congress a more effective partner in trade policy. The president should support the establishment of this office to improve congressional involvement in trade policymaking. The CTO would help members at the personal and committee levels gain a better understanding of the benefits and costs of trade agreements.

Moreover, the CTO would enable Congress to develop a greater understanding of the trade barriers confronting America's exports and imports in the 21st century. Finally, such an office would aid members with many different responsibilities to better participate in trade policymaking.

RECOMMENDATIONS

- The president should propose to Congress the designation of USTR as a cabinet-level Department of Trade to more effectively develop, monitor, articulate, and enforce trade policies.
- To further this process, Congress should establish, with the president's support, a Congressional Trade Office.

NOTES

1. Susan Ariel Aaronson, *Trade and the American Dream: A Social History of Postwar Trade Policy* (Lexington, KY: University Press of Kentucky, 1996), pp. 21, 31.

2. Stephen P. Haggard, "Foundations of Hegemony," in *The State and American Foreign Economic Policy*, ed. G. John Ikenberry et al. (Ithaca, NY: Cornell University Press, 1988), pp. 112-113.

3. On distrust of the State Department, see Aaronson, *Trade and the American Dream*, pp. 36, 110, fn. 38; on formation of the Special Trade Representative, see I.M. Destler, *American Trade Politics,* 3rd ed. (Washington, DC: IIE, 1995), p. 108.

4. Destler, *American Trade Politics,* pp. 108-117, quotation on p. 117.

5. Ibid., pp. 119-120.

6. Susan Ariel Aaronson, *Taking Trade to the Streets: The Lost History of Public Efforts to Shape Globalization* (Ann Arbor: University of Michigan Press, 2001), pp. 110-141.

7. Destler, *American Trade Politics,* pp. 132-137.

8. Congress approved NAFTA and the Uruguay Round by significant majorities.

9. Ambassador Charlene Barshefsky, "The Record and the Road Ahead," speech to the Democratic Leadership Council, December 14, 2000; and Ambassador Barshefsky, "Thoughts at a Moment of Transition," speech at the Economic Strategy Institute, December 19, 2000.

10. I.M Destler, *The National Economic Council: A Work in Progress* (Washington, DC: IIE, 1998), p. 13. On Bush's trade policy, see "Whoduzzit," *The Economist,* March 3, 2001, pp. 28-29.

11. GAO, Report to the Chairman, Committee on Ways and Means, U.S. House, "International Trade: Improvements Needed to Track and Archive Trade Agreements" (GAO/NSIAD-00-24, December 14, 1999).

12. GAO, Report to the Chairman, Committee on Ways and Means, U.S. House, "International Trade: Strategy Needed to Better Monitor and Enforce Trade Agreements" (GAO/NSIAD-00-76, March 2000), pp. 1-15.

13. Ibid., pp. 19, 26-28.

14. Randy Mikkelsen, "Bush Picks Zoellick as US Trade Rep," Reuters, January 11, 2001; and Steven Pearlstein, "Trade Representative to Keep Rank," *Washington Post,* January 13, 2001.

4

Revamping the Role of Congress in Trade Policy

by Ira Wolf
Senior Advisor on Trade Policy to Senator Max Baucus (D-MT)

THE PROBLEM

C ongress is not well organized or adequately staffed to make trade policy. Article I of the Constitution establishes Congress and states that "Congress shall have the power . . . to regulate commerce with foreign nations . . . and to lay and collect . . . duties." The presidency is established in Article II, yet is given no trade authority. Thus, it is clear that the Constitution gives Congress the central authority to regulate trade. Over the past half century, Congress has delegated significant authority on trade policy to the executive branch. Yet Congress retains considerable power and interest in trade issues and wants to play a more active role.

Over the years, citizens have heard complaints that an unsophisticated Congress, with 535 "wanna be" secretaries of state, is interfering with and damaging the proper management of American foreign policy. The same complaints are increasingly heard about trade policy today. These accusations represent an unrequited hope that the world can return to a time when policy issues were managed without the involvement of interest groups, nongovernmental organizations, and average citizens, along with the absence of serious scrutiny by the media. That era is over. We need to ensure that the foundation for the new and broader participation in trade policy, including that of Congress, is properly established.

The Democratic commissioners on the U.S. Trade Deficit Review Commission wrote: "Congressional efforts to carry out this mandate [develop trade policy and regulate foreign commerce] are hampered by a splintered framework for handling trade issues and limited resources to do so. Committees with primary jurisdiction for trade issues can't address the increasingly broad array of issues that are now inherent in U.S. trade policy."[1]

BACKGROUND

Congress must address four central challenges to improve and modernize its role in trade policymaking. First, there is an imbalance between the legislative branch and the executive branch in terms of the resources devoted to trade. I am not suggesting that the two branches of government should have equal resources, as Congress does not negotiate, implement, or enforce trade agreements. But Congress sets the direction for the nation's trade policy. It establishes trade priorities. It has the power to reduce tariffs and alter or eliminate nontariff barriers. As international trade negotiations increasingly involve domestic regulatory issues, Congress has the power to change the laws. Congress exerts oversight on how the executive branch implements trade policy and enforces trade laws. Thus, Congress needs significant professional trade expertise to perform these functions, and this expertise is insufficient today.

Second, there is an imbalance within Congress in trade expertise. Through the early 1980s, only a small number of congressional staff members had knowledge and experience in the trade area. Today, almost every Senator and House member has at least one staff aide who follows trade issues closely. In fact, a number of Senators and House members are themselves genuine trade experts. As Americans' interest in trade-related issues has expanded, members of Congress have responded by increasing their focus and upgrading their expertise. The result is that individual Americans and interest groups now have multiple points of access through Congress to the national trade policymaking process. This increased participation in the public policy process is good for the country. But effective policymaking requires that these hundreds of discrete access points in Congress be aggregated.

In the past, the Senate Finance Committee and the House Ways and Means Committee were the focal points where these views were brought together into a coherent whole. Legislation originated with those committees and then moved to the floor for general debate and passage. Yet, the present size of their trade staffs is essentially the same as it was 15 years ago. Thus, an imbalance is growing within Congress between those who propound specific interests and those who have the role of drawing together those interests into a broader national policy and legislation.

Third, many issues that have not traditionally been linked with trade are now being addressed at the World Trade Organization. Some of these issues are already central to the WTO process, such as intellectual property rights, industrial standards, and food safety.

Others are now being discussed at the WTO, or on its periphery, and may become subject to WTO disciplines in the future. This list includes the environment, genetically modified organisms, health, labor rights, competition policy, and electronic commerce. Many of the issues fall, at the first instance, under the jurisdiction of congressional committees that have never been involved in trade policy, trade law, or trade negotiations. The committees' staffs have had no reason to develop trade expertise, much less the need to understand how the purely domestic regulatory issues they have traditionally dealt with are now part of international trade. How will the members of the committees and their staffs address this intersection of trade with these domestic regulatory issues?

Fourth, congressional observation and monitoring of trade negotiations is weak. In recent years, few members of Congress or congressional staff have observed negotiations and discussions at the WTO. However, 100 members of Congress went to the WTO ministerial in Seattle in December 1999. One important example of recent inadequate activity was the critically important negotiations with China in Geneva on that country's accession to the WTO. No congressional staff attended to observe, monitor, and report on those sessions.

The 1988 Trade Act created a formal group of Congressional Trade Advisors, five from the Senate and five from the House. In recent years, however, this group has been dormant.

Trade is just one of the many public policies that busy members of Congress must decide upon. At a minimum, their expert staff should be attending selected key multilateral and bilateral negotiations and consultations. This is not to suggest that congressional staff, or members of Congress when they participate, be allowed to negotiate. But someone who is accountable to members of Congress needs to observe trade negotiations, follow the process over time, and report back.

SOLUTIONS

Senator Max Baucus (D-MT) has proposed a Congressional Trade Office in Senate bill S. 2226, introduced on February 7, 2001. The CTO would provide Congress with additional independent, nonpartisan, and neutral trade expertise. It would enable more members of Congress to meet their trade responsibilities. Moreover, Congress might be more willing to grant authority to the executive if it had greater

ability to monitor trade agreements negotiated by the executive. Such
an institution is not unprecedented. In the past, Congress has created
similar institutions, such as the Congressional Budget Office.

Functions of the Congressional Trade Office

The CTO would be charged with monitoring compliance with
major bilateral, regional, and global trade agreements. The first step
in effective compliance is to keep adequate records regarding these
agreements. As GAO noted in a December 1999 study, there are
recordkeeping weaknesses and inconsistencies in the archives of the
U.S. Trade Representative and the Departments of Commerce and
State. In addition, Congress may not have received all of the agreements and accompanying documents, as required by law.
Furthermore, the public does not have comprehensive and ready
access to all trade agreements.[2]

In its March 2000 report, the GAO noted that "the expertise
needed to analyze compliance problems is not always available."[3] The
Republican commissioners on the U.S. Trade Deficit Review
Commission called for greater staffing and enforcement of compliance with trade agreements.[4] But Congress must have its own staff to
monitor trade agreements because negotiators may not be able to
provide an objective assessment of agreements.

Second, CTO staff should participate as observers in key trade
negotiations. CTO staff would also observe selected WTO and other
dispute settlement panel deliberations as official members of the U.S.
government delegation. Again, Congress needs an independent
assessment of ongoing trade negotiations and of the dispute settlement process that is so important in maintaining support for trade
agreements.

Third, the CTO would analyze administration trade initiatives.
This includes analysis of selected proposed trade agreements and
trade policy actions. The office would analyze the trade accounts
each quarter, including the global current account, the global trade
account, and key bilateral trade accounts. After the administration
delivers its annual National Trade Estimates Report to Congress, the
CTO would analyze the major outstanding trade barriers based on
the cost to the U.S. economy. It would also provide an analysis of the
administration's Trade Policy Agenda. Further, the office would examine the actual impact of trade agreements upon American business.

Fourth, CTO staff would assist committees that do not have traditional trade-related responsibilities in understanding the working of the WTO and other multilateral institutions that have an impact on domestic regulatory issues.

Structure of the CTO
The CTO should be responsible to the Senate Finance Committee and the House Ways and Means Committee. The director of the CTO would be appointed by the chairmen and ranking minority members of both committees. At the same time, the CTO would service other committees involved in trade issues as described above.

The staff would consist of a minimum of 10 professionals with expertise in geographic regions (Asia, Europe, Latin America, and Africa), functions (trade economics, trade law, intellectual property rights, e-commerce, labor, and environment), and industries (high tech, basic industries, and services). To develop an institutional memory, so important in trade negotiations, these professionals would be encouraged through financial incentives to remain with the office for a long period of time. As trade issues become increasingly complex, long-term, in-depth knowledge about trade policy and trade negotiations will be even more necessary than in the past.

Some might argue that Congress has outside agencies to do these multiple tasks. The Congressional Research Service focuses on issues before Congress in the current session. The U.S. International Trade Commission, an independent agency, is slow and not policy-oriented. The GAO conducts thorough and lengthy examinations of issues, but it can handle only a small number at a time.

Other analysts and scholars have proposed different strategies for modernizing congressional trade policymaking. For example, Bruce Stokes, Senior Fellow at the Council on Foreign Relations, has suggested a Joint Committee on Trade consisting of the chairmen and ranking members of those committees and subcommittees with functions related to trade.[5] However, this would require a major change in the committee structure of Congress. The CTO, in contrast, would not change how Congress works or limit the participants in trade policymaking. It is the most effective approach to help Congress meet its constitutionally mandated responsibilities in the 21st century.

RECOMMENDATION
- Congress should approve legislation creating a Congressional Trade Office.

NOTES

1. U.S. Trade Deficit Review Commission, *The U.S. Trade Deficit: Causes, Consequences and Recommendations for Action* (Washington, DC: The Commission, November 14, 2000), p. 206.

2. GAO, Report to the Chairman, Committee on Ways and Means, U.S. House, "International Trade: Improvements Needed to Track and Archive Trade Agreements" (GAO/NSIAD-00-24, December 14, 1999).

3. GAO, Report to the Chairman, Committee on Ways and Means, U.S. House, "International Trade: Strategy Needed to Better Monitor and Enforce Trade Agreements" (GAO/NSIAD-00-76, March 2000), p. 5.

4. U.S. Trade Deficit Review Commission, *The U.S. Trade Deficit*, p. 223.

5. Bruce Stokes, *National Journal*, February 3, 2001, p. 357.

5

Strategies to Involve New Groups
in Trade Policymaking

THE PROBLEM

W ho has the ear of the U.S. Trade Representative? In general, advisors to USTR represent economic interests that have a direct stake in U.S. trade policy. In recent years, however, new groups with indirect and often noneconomic interests in trade policy have sought to participate in advising the U.S. government on trade. These groups include democracy, human rights, environmental, science, developmental, public health, and consumer activists. The George H. Bush and William J. Clinton administrations broadened the advisory committee structure to reflect a wider range of interests. But having more committees with more members does not necessarily yield better trade policies. Some groups argue that the advisory system remains too focused on U.S. commercial and economic interests rather than on a broader conception of the national interest in promoting trade. In addition, federal courts have ruled that the current advisory committee process is not in compliance with federal law and must be revamped. As USTR rethinks who should advise the U.S. government on trade, it should also reexamine how it involves these advisors in the development of trade policy. Finally, the government has yet to fully tap new technologies to solicit broader public opinion on trade.

BACKGROUND

USTR

In 1934, when Congress first authorized the executive to participate in bilateral trade agreements, it formalized a process by which the public could have input into trade policymaking. It created the Committee on Reciprocity Information to hold hearings on the views of interested parties. However, the committee was composed solely of government officials. While it sought public input, it tended to listen to the traditional constituents of trade: farm, business, and labor leaders. As a result, some members of Congress as well as citizens criticized the advisory process and urged that it be broadened to include a wider variety of views.[1]

As trade became more important to various sectors of the U.S. economy and as policymakers began to expand the scope of the GATT to include more than commercial policy (in particular, nontariff trade barriers), business leaders began to complain that they did not have enough influence on negotiators and negotiations. Congress thus established a new advisory committee system in 1974 to ensure that U.S. trade policy and trade negotiation objectives adequately reflected U.S. commercial and economic interests. The Special Trade Representative developed a general advisory committee as well as sector-specific advisory committees. According to I.M. Destler, "Each committee was broad enough . . . to encompass a range of firms and interests. Their exposure to one another gave committee members a broader perspective, and it gave executive officials useful leeway on whose advice they finally took. And because the advisors felt they were taken seriously—and came to understand the constraints faced by their governmental counterparts—they developed sympathy for the larger enterprise."[2] The very process of seeking input helped build a constituency for trade. Over time, the advisory committees became advocates for the larger cause of economic internationalism. But trade officials did not effectively use the advisory system to build a broader public constituency in support of economic internationalism. The circle of individuals making trade policy remained small.

While Congress expanded and enhanced the advisory committee system in three subsequent trade acts, it did not require negotiators to obtain input from individuals or groups with an indirect economic or noneconomic stake in trade. By the 1990s, however, policymakers recognized that new groups such as environmentalists and human rights activists were increasingly concerned about trade. The George H. Bush administration was the first to welcome input from environmentalists in trade policymaking. The Clinton administration created a special Trade and Environmental Policy Committee to give USTR advice on the nexus between trade and the environment; its members come from industry, agriculture, consumer, and environmental groups.[3] During this period as well, the main advisory committees began to include the views of state and local officials on trade.

The U.S. Advisory Committee Structure and Process

Today, the advisory committees provide information and advice on U.S. negotiating objectives and bargaining positions before the United States enters into trade agreements, on the operation of any trade agreement once entered into, and on other matters arising in connection with the development, implementation, and administration of trade policy. Because of the import and scope of goods and services that America trades, the advisory system has grown into a vast administrative structure of 33 committees and 1,000 advisors.[4]

There are three tiers of trade policy advisors (see the box for a listing of the committees). The most important advisory body is the Advisory Committee for Trade Policy and Negotiations (ACTPN.) The president appoints 45 ACTPN members for two-year terms. The 1974 Trade Act requires that the membership represent the key economic sectors affected by trade and not the wide range of national concerns that trade impacts. However, ACTPN is charged with considering trade policy issues in the context of the overall national interest.[5] Moreover, USTR must weigh economic interests against broad political, social, and environmental interests in obtaining advice.

The second tier includes the six policy advisory committees appointed by the USTR alone or in conjunction with the Departments of Agriculture, Labor, and Defense and the Environmental Protection

---

ADVISORY COMMITTEES

USTR-Administered Committees
Advisory Committee for Trade Policy and Negotiations (ACTPN)
Intergovernmental Policy Advisory Committee (IGPAC)
Trade Advisory Committee for Africa (TACA)
USTR and Environmental Protection Agency-Administered Committee
Trade and Environment Policy Advisory Committee (TEPAC)
USTR and Department of Labor-Administered Committee
Labor Advisory Committee (LAC)
USTR and Department of Defense-Administered Committee
Defense Policy Advisory Committee for Trade (DPACT)
USTR and Department of Agriculture-Administered Committees
Agricultural Policy Advisory Committee for Trade (APAC)
Agricultural Technical Advisory Committee for Trade (ATAC) (5 subcommittees)
USTR and Department of Commerce-Administered Committee
Industry Functional Advisory Committee (IFAC) (18 IFACs)

Agency. Each committee provides advice based on the perspective of its specific area.

The third level of advisors incorporates 26 sectorial, technical, and functional committees that are organized into two areas: industry and agriculture. Members are appointed jointly by USTR and the Secretaries of Commerce and Agriculture. Each sectorial or technical committee represents a sector or commodity group, such as textiles or dairy products, and offers technical advice on the possible effects of trade policy on its sector. Four functional committees give cross-sectorial advice on customs, standards, intellectual property, and electronic commerce.[6]

Recommendations for committee membership come from a number of sources, including Congress, associations, organizations, and individuals with an interest or expertise in trade policy. The Federal Advisory Committee Act of 1972 requires that committee members reflect the mix of the U.S. population, different economic sectors, large and small businesses, and the diversity of civil society groups.

The Government's Continuing Problems in Getting Good Advice

Politics (and campaign contributions) have influenced the selection of members. During the Clinton administration, it became evident that several individuals on key advisory committees had raised or donated significant funds to the Clinton campaign or the Democratic party.[7] Was membership on an advisory committee the payoff for a contribution? Other administrations may also have given advisory slots to campaign donors. Such a strategy may make political sense, but does little to ensure that the president gets good information to make trade policy.

This has not been the only controversy confronting the advisory process. In July 1999, Earthjustice, the Sierra Club, and other environmental groups filed a lawsuit in Federal District Court in Seattle accusing the advisory committees of excluding environmentalists. The district court directed the U.S. government to include environmentalists on all advisory committees.[8]

The Clinton administration developed proposals to revamp the advisory committee structure. It remains to be seen whether the Bush administration will adopt or alter those recommendations. The Clinton administration also changed the procedures for advisory committee meetings, allowing part of them to be open to the public.

Any secret preliminary proposals are not discussed during the open portion of the meeting. Despite these changes, the advisory committees do not reflect the wide range of noneconomic concerns about the course of trade policy. According to Jon Huenemann, former assistant USTR for North America, the advisory system "is not designed to efficiently and decisively deal with fundamental concerns about the overall open market objectives of U.S. trade policy."[9]

USTR has not used the advisory committees to anticipate new concerns about trade agreements. Moreover, USTR has not created advisory committees on controversial issues such as genetically modified foods or global public health. It has, however, responded to the loudest and most politically effective trade agreements critics by including some on advisory committees. Even so, USTR's approach to the committees has been responsive rather than proactive. The majority of advisors continue to be individuals with direct economic stakes in the process.

USTR does not effectively use the Internet to solicit public opinion about trade. The government first communicated trade policy on the Internet in 1997, when the White House set up a fast track site. USTR also developed a Web site, but it was neither searchable nor linked to other sites. It was merely a repository of government documents and did not explain the functions of USTR or the importance of trade agreements to America and Americans. In 2000, through a major gift from a private donor, USTR's site and many other government sites were revamped. Nevertheless, USTR's site remains strictly a dissemination device and is not interactive. It is now searchable, however, and its outreach page has links to various trade advisory committees and relevant federal register notes, as well as links to general information about trade.[10]

Other Nations' Advisory Approaches

Canada and the European Union, among other countries, have advisory systems similar to that of the United States. But their approaches involve a broader cross section of individuals in the advisory process and more effectively engage and inform the public on trade issues than does the United States. As Jon Huenemann notes, Mexico has a two-tier advisory system: the first is business-based; the second includes peasants, academics, small farmers, and industrial workers. The Mexican government pays their travel and other expenses, which allows members to meet every two months. In contrast, the U.S. government does not fund travel for advisory committee members, which makes it easier for those with an economic stake in trade to justify attendance at the meetings. Canada has a federal and provincial advisory system and holds public hearings on important trade issues throughout the country.[11]

Further, some governments, such as the Canadian and the Australian, use their trade ministry Web sites much more effectively than does the United States to educate their constituents and other interested parties. The European Union's Commissioner for Trade, for example, regularly engages in an interactive dialogue on the Web with interested citizens.

SOLUTIONS

USTR must make clear the functions of its advisors and how it should use their advice, as Phyllis Bonanno, Assistant USTR for Public Liaison in the George H. Bush Administration, has suggested.[12] The structure and objectives of the advisory committees need clarification from Congress. USTR should press for legislation to allow it to seek advice and feedback from noneconomic interests and to make their views a negotiating priority. This will ensure that U.S. trade policy is built on a broad base of public support. According to some critics, USTR does not need formal committees for good advice. Indeed, some argue that the advisory committees should be abandoned so that special interests do not have additional opportunity to present their views to negotiators.

The Web can be a cost- and labor-effective way to inform citizens about trade policy and to seek their input. Mark Ritchie, President of the Institute for Agriculture and Trade Policy and a member of the Trade and Environment Policy Advisory Committee, recommends that USTR seek public comment on its trade policy proposals on the Web, as Canada does. USTR should use the Web to relate trade policy to peoples' daily lives, to explain how Americans as taxpayers, consumers, producers, citizens, and friends of the earth are constantly affected by trade. USTR could Web-cast town hall meetings on trade or the open portion of advisory committee meetings. USTR would thereby be telling American citizens that their views on trade matter.

Through the Internet (as well as other new technologies), USTR could facilitate trade negotiations. Cleared advisors would receive up-to-date information and communicate directly, even instantaneously, with negotiators. Negotiators would be able to respond rapidly to offers and negotiating ploys from other governments. Secure Web sites and Web conferencing could, over time, shorten the duration of trade negotiations, which are notoriously time-consuming and staff-intensive. Furthermore, Web-casting certain speeches at the negotiations might reduce some of the public's concern about secrecy and help build confidence in trade officials. With a better understanding of the negotiation process, citizens might be more supportive of the outcome.

Nonetheless, the Internet by itself cannot ensure a better understanding of trade policy. Leaders in government, business, labor, and civil society must encourage more comprehensive discussions of trade at the local and national levels. The Internet can amplify these debates and involve a broader cross section of Americans in the trade discussions in a timely manner.

On balance, USTR should not abandon the advisory committees, but use them as one of several channels to obtain the public's input. USTR should also get feedback from public hearings, an interactive Web site, members of Congress, and cleared advisors.

RECOMMENDATIONS

- The structure and objectives of the advisory committees must be clarified. USTR should propose legislation that will empower it to seek advice not just from U.S. commercial and economic interests, but also from consumer, environmental, public health, and other broad national interests.
- USTR's Web site should become interactive. USTR should use the Internet to obtain the public's input and to present information on trade in a labor- and cost-efficient manner. USTR should also use the Web to facilitate discussions with cleared trade advisors to promote instantaneous and broader debates during the negotiating process.
- In addition to the Internet, USTR should turn to public hearings, Congress, and the advisory committees to solicit public opinion on trade policymaking.

NOTES

1. John Day Larkin, *Trade Agreements: A Study in Democratic Methods* (New York: Columbia University, 1940), pp. 6-48; and Henry J. Tasca, *The Reciprocal Trade Policy of the United States: A Study in Trade Philosophy* (Philadelphia: University of Pennsylvania Press, 1938), p. 290.

2. I.M. Destler, *American Trade Politics* (Washington, DC: IIE, 1995), 3rd ed., p. 112.

3. John J. Audley, *Green Politics and Global Trade: NAFTA and the Future of Environmental Politics* (Washington, DC: Georgetown University Press, 1997), p. 125.

4. www.ustr.gov/outreach/advise.shtml.

5. Ibid.

6. Ibid.

7. Author's interview with Phyllis Shearer Jones, former Assistant USTR for Public Liaison, March 4, 1998; and www.ustr.gov/outreach/advise.shtml.

8. Author's interview with Phyllis Shearer Jones, March 27, 2001.

9. Jon Huenemann, "Nongovernment Actors and the Making of Trade Policy," *Looking Ahead* (Vol. XXIII, No. 1), April 2001, p. 3. The article is based on Mr. Huenemann's presentation at NPA's fifth trade seminar held in February 2001. He is currently Vice President, GPC International.

10. www.ustr.gov/outreach/index.shtml.

11. Huenemann, "Nongovernment Actors."

12. Memorandum from Phyllis O. Bonanno to Susan Aaronson, February 25, 2001.

6

Building Greater Public Understanding
of Trade Policy

THE PROBLEM

F or some 60 years, policymakers have justified U.S. participation in trade agreements by citing the economic benefits of trade. They have argued that trade creates high wage jobs, yields domestic economic growth, and helps cement global peace and stability. In general, policymakers have made macroeconomic arguments in support of trade and trade agreements. These arguments, however, have not sold the American people on trade agreements. While Americans support trade, they think that big business and not citizens are the key beneficiaries. Moreover, a strong majority of Americans believe that trade agreements do not adequately incorporate concerns about labor standards and the environment.[1] How can policymakers talk about trade agreements so that the American public will listen? How can citizens gain a greater understanding of what trade agreements can and cannot do?

BACKGROUND

My neighborhood of Arlington, Virginia, is much like other U.S. suburbs. The people on my block work hard, save for their children's education, and look forward to their retirement. They rarely think about trade policy. Yet trade policy is an integral part of their daily lives. My neighbors, like other Americans, drink French wine, eat Mexican food, and work on computers made in Malaysia. They save for college or retirement by investing in American companies that import goods, in American companies that sell goods overseas, and in foreign companies that invest in the United States. When they shop, they load up their Fords and Hondas with many products, some of which are made overseas.

Like most Americans, my neighbors rarely connect trade policy to what they do and how they do it. Mike, my next door neighbor, markets Georgetown University's basketball team. Some of the team's uniforms, like some of the team's top players, are imported. Sandra, who lives across the street, is a prosecutor. She often prosecutes major drug cases involving individuals who have brought illegal drugs into the United States. Like Mike, she rarely thinks about trade policy. Jeff, who lives on the corner, owns a dry-cleaning operation where many Washington hotels send their linen. His job is to guarantee that Washington's visitors, many of whom come from abroad, eat and sleep on fresh linen. But he does not see how his business relates to trade. In contrast, Sam, who lives two doors away, is very worried about trade policy. As an economist for a labor union, he closely monitors how Washington policies affect people on the shop floor who produce goods for home markets and for export. My neighbors know that the United States is the world's most active trading nation, but they are more aware that the United States is relatively self-sufficient in many products. They tend to believe that trade agreements free trade and allow other nations to trade unfairly. Although they have heard clichés about the "global village," most of my neighbors do not think they live there. Yet they do—there is no other "village" they can move to. Because we live in the global village, we want all of its citizens to adhere to a uniform set of rules that govern transactions between citizens of different nations. An increasing number of the rules to govern globalization are embodied within trade agreements.

The United States is a signatory to some 400 trade agreements. In recent years, these agreements have had a significant impact on the U.S. and global economies. They have helped American and foreign companies build global market share, producing enormous economies of scale and scope that have lowered prices for consumers in the United States and around the world. But many Americans are not cognizant of these benefits. They have heard a great deal about the costs of the huge U.S. trade deficit, but little about how both imports as well as exports stimulate economic growth.[2] They have heard even less about how trade agreements help regulate trade between nations with different economies, political systems, and norms.

Why the Public Misunderstands Trade

Policymakers bear much of the blame for the public's misunderstanding of trade agreements. They have not effectively communicated why such agreements are essential, nor have they adequately explained what trade agreements do.

NAFTA is an example of the failure to communicate the rationale for trade agreements. The George H. Bush administration saw NAFTA as a lever to encourage Mexico's continued pursuit of market-oriented policies. The administration hoped that as Mexico experienced greater economic growth, fewer Mexicans might migrate illegally to the United States; with less competition from illegal aliens, low skilled U.S. workers might find greater opportunities and even higher wages. But the Bush and later Clinton administrations did not discuss all of these reasons in talking about the potential agreement to the American people.[3] The public debate over NAFTA was essentially a fight about the number of jobs that NAFTA would create or destroy.

Policymakers and the public had a broader debate about the WTO, "colored by very real concerns that the United States could lose control of its health, environmental, workplace, and safety standards."[4] Yet much of the debate was simplistic. Opponents linked the new WTO (and NAFTA) to the interests of big business and not to the interests of average Americans. The Clinton administration responded by defending the WTO, arguing that high wage, high skilled jobs created by demand from emerging markets would keep the American dream alive. That argument was effective on Capitol Hill. The Uruguay Round (and the WTO) received a resounding vote of support in both Houses of Congress. But the public still did not understand its stake in trade agreements.

To win congressional support for NAFTA and the WTO, the Clinton administration traded "pork" and unrelated legislation. Some vote-buying may always be necessary. However, by trading pork for votes in these cases, the administration undermined the political and economic rationale for trade agreements. The administration's strategy convinced many critics that trade policy was also undermining the achievement of other important policy goals. The failure to communicate the rationale for trade agreements became crucial when the Clinton administration decided to host a ministerial meeting of the WTO in the United States to kick off a new round of multinational trade liberalization.

The Clinton administration had debated for years whether to host a trade ministerial. While some officials argued that a ministerial would build support for trade, others feared that it would weaken U.S. support for the WTO. Notwithstanding the Geneva celebration of the 50th anniversary of the GATT in 1998 where massive and violent street protests occurred, the president decided that the United States should host the meeting.

President Clinton did not want to undermine the ministerial by encouraging a congressional debate about whether the United States should host it, let alone whether the United States should pay for it. Thus, the administration told the host city, Seattle, that it must develop a committee to raise funds to support the ministerial. However, all previous ministerials and GATT rounds had been financed by the host government and the GATT/WTO.

Seattle appeared to be a good choice, given the city's long and broad interest in trade, its diverse economic base, and its strong union history. But because of the administration's reliance on corporate support for the ministerial, some critics alleged that the meeting was the Boeing/Microsoft ministerial. It is true that many of the firms called on to support the ministerial were the same companies that might benefit from trade talks if such talks succeeded. Yet, the administration did not foresee any potential conflict of interest. In addition, many observers viewed the administration's negotiating priorities on agriculture and e-commerce as designed to benefit key political constituencies of the Democrats. Critics charged that the fox was funding and guarding the chicken coop, leaving the people outside. The administration's stance also furthered the impression that the only beneficiaries of trade liberalization were big business and major shareholders.

The administration did not do a good job in preparing the public for the ministerial. Both the Agriculture Department and USTR held hearings around the country. However, while USTR officials "heard" what the public was saying about trade agreements, they did not change USTR's negotiating priorities and procedures. USTR did not use the hearings or the ministerial as an opportunity to educate Americans about the costs and benefits of trade agreements or what trade agreements do.

When approximately 30,000 people took to the streets for days to protest the ministerial, Americans had to wonder why these people were so angry. The Seattle ministerial certainly did not enhance the public's image of the WTO or trade. Moreover, protestors' complaints about the secrecy of the negotiations resonated with the public. The closed door nature of the negotiations led credence to protestors' allegations that many Americans would not approve of what was happening.

SOLUTIONS

Trade agreements are America's main tool to govern globalization, a phenomenon that frightens many Americans. To address their fears, policymakers must promote a different discussion about trade and trade agreements. Americans need such knowledge because trade is a huge and growing percentage of gross domestic product—about 27 percent. Furthermore, trade policies increasingly affect the achievement of other policy goals, from public health to immigration to patent policies. This fact alone is stimulating a different debate about trade policy.

In recent months, the WTO dispute settlement body has made major decisions on tax and environmental policies, issues of concern to many Americans. Some business leaders and environmentalists argue that the United States should not "cave in" to WTO decisions; others see these decisions as an opportunity to improve public policies—to ensure that such policies promote a more universal approach to, for example, protecting the environment without distorting trade. Policymakers recognize that America does not have to change its policies in response to any WTO decision. Nonetheless, if the U.S. government does not alter public policies that the WTO deems may distort trade, the United States may have to pay compensatory damages or accept retaliation from its trading partners.

Environmentalists, human rights, and development activists are now key actors in trade policymaking. The involvement of new groups in a more diverse debate about trade agreements, however, has not resulted in a more informed debate.

While dissent on trade is not new, Americans seem unable to find consensus on U.S. negotiating objectives for trade agreements. Ironically, at the same time, they use trade policy in an attempt to achieve too many policy goals. In recent years, the United States has used trade policy to protect sea turtles, to prevent the spread of diseases such as mad cow, and to sustain certain sectors such as sugar farmers and steel producers. Policymakers have also turned to trade policy to punish rogue nations like Iraq, to lower pharmaceutical costs for AIDS victims in certain developing countries (but not at home), and to ensure that countries protect the intellectual property of Americans such as Madonna and Microsoft. The utilization of trade policy to do so many tasks foments confusion about trade and undermines support for trade agreements.

Why does the United States rely so heavily on trade policy to address globalization? First, trade policies give America enormous leverage around the world because so many nations want to trade with the United States. Second, trade policy is off budget. Policymakers do not need specific budget allocations to lower pharmaceutical costs for AIDS victims or to subsidize the steel industry. Nevertheless, if the United States wants to expand trade agreements and to build public support for them, officials must ask whether trade policy is the best and most cost-effective policy solution for these problems.

How can policymakers get the public to focus on trade policy when people can barely juggle their work and family lives, let alone the many other public policy issues that call for their attention? With the recognition that neither trade policy nor civics is taught in most high schools, policymakers should take every opportunity to speak to their constituents about trade. To get people to listen, policymakers must be honest about the benefits and costs of trade agreements, explain what the United States really does in negotiating them, and, finally, make a case for trade that people can relate to.

Trade agreement proponents and opponents alike should:

Highlight the rationale for trade. No one trades unless they perceive mutual benefit, but the notion of benefit seems lost from the trade debate. When we travel to Paris or Casablanca or Sydney on a honeymoon, we voluntarily choose to trade. When we choose between a U.S.-made Honda or a Korean-made Hyundai, we choose to trade or not to trade. The citizen is in the driver's seat.

Explain what trade agreements do. Trade agreements regulate how firms may trade and when nations may protect. They are one of several tools with which policymakers regulate global markets. Citizens, producers, friends of the earth, consumers, shareholders, and taxpayers need these regulations to encourage economic efficiency and to discourage policymakers from frequently resorting to protection because of domestic political pressures. Moreover, citizens need such regulations because global markets, like domestic markets, produce market failures, as when the price or supply of goods does not accurately reflect the cost to the environment or when some producers gain unfair market share. Trade agreements, like domestic regulations, are often imperfect and incomplete, and they come with costs to some producers and consumers. Thus, trade agreements must be frequently renegotiated. Trade ministerials, such as the November 9-13, 2001, meeting of the WTO in Doha, Qatar, present an opportunity to begin a different dialogue on trade.

Explain how trade affects Americans in their daily lives. Every hour of every day, Americans see, smell, touch, taste, and hear goods and services that are traded between the United States and other nations. Americans' perspective on trade policy may stem from how trade most affects them whether as consumer, producer, shareholder, friend of the earth, or taxpayer. However, their conclusions about trade policy may turn out differently if they examine the costs and benefits of trade from each of those perspectives. One can simultaneously be a winner and a loser from trade agreements. By understanding how trade affects their daily lives, people are empowered.

Encourage a more honest and complete discussion about trade as well as alternative or complementary tools to govern globalization. Be honest about the potential and the limitations of trade agreements. As citizens learn how trade affects them, they may become more supportive of the need to develop trade agreements and better able to see the potential and the limitations of such agreements. This knowledge should, over time, help Americans understand whether trade agreements are the only or best policy tool to encourage the protection of human rights and the preservation of the global commons as well as other policy goals.

RECOMMENDATIONS

To talk about trade so that Americans will listen, policymakers must:

- Highlight the rationale for trade.
- Explain what trade agreements do—they are one of several tools with which policymakers govern globalization.
- Explain how trade affects Americans in their daily lives.
- Encourage a more honest and complete discussion about trade as well as alternative and complementary tools to govern globalization.

NOTES

1. Program on International Policy Attitudes, "Americans on Globalization," poll conducted October 21-October 29, 1999, with 18,126 adults. See www.pipa.org/OnlineReports/Globalization/executive_summary.html; and "Globalization: What Americans Are Worried About," *Business Week*/Harris Poll, *Business Week*, April 24, 2000, p. 44.

2. Council of Economic Advisors, *Economic Report of the President: Transmitted to the Congress, February 1994* (Washington, DC: GPO, 1994), pp. 268-269; and U.S. Trade Representative, *1999 Annual Report* (Washington, DC: GPO, 2000), p. 2.

3. Bruce Michael Bagley, "U.S. Policy Toward Mexico," in *Mexico and the United States: Managing the Relationship,* ed. Riordan Roett (Boulder, CO: Westview Press, 1988), p. 224.

4. Susan Ariel Aaronson, *Trade and the American Dream: A Social History of Postwar Trade Policy* (Lexington, KY: University Press of Kentucky, 1996), p. 173.

7

Looking Back on NPA's Trade Seminars

by Paul Magnusson
Washington Correspondent, *BusinessWeek*, and moderator,
NPA Trade Seminars

W hen U.S. Trade Representative Robert B. Zoellick debated the Bush administration's trade policy before the House Ways and Means Committee in March 2001, the faces in the audience told the real story. Business lobbyists sat beside environmental activists and labor officials. The ornate walls of the cavernous hearing room were lined with people worried about globalization, worker rights, religious freedom, rainforest destruction, biodiversity, global warming, intellectual property rights, medical research, animal welfare, and a dozen other issues. At two long tables, 40 journalists hunched over written statements from members of the committee, Ambassador Zoellick's carefully hedged written testimony, and propaganda handouts from the pressure groups throughout the room.

As a matter of public interest, international trade is suddenly big. The topic has become a lightening rod for every criticism of free market capitalism, every concern about the effect of humans on the environment, and every worry about nationalism, sovereignty, and local rule—for good reason. Subsistence farmers in Madagascar are affected by export subsidies provided European farmers. Fishermen casting their nets in Thailand are affected by a treaty reached in Canada to protect sea turtles. AIDS sufferers in South Africa may live or die according to copyright agreements reached in Switzerland. Like a parade, international trade invites people advocating all manner of causes to pick up their banners and march along.

So Zoellick's speech and the solemn statements of members of Congress sounded more like pages torn from an Ionesco play in which the characters talk past each other. Official Washington debated this seemingly radical idea: whether future trade agreements among nations might acknowledge that trillions of dollars worth of goods and services and currency traveling around the globe might indeed have some profound effect on the environment and on the rights and quality of the lives of workers.

Congress and the administration are now like two people stumbling around in a dark room looking for the light switch. But the room is actually a set on a stage, and the audience is shouting contradictory instructions to them. No wonder they are confused.

FINDING COMMON GROUND

It was the intent of the series of trade seminars sponsored by the National Policy Association to give those two a little help in finding the switch by identifying some common instructions among the audience. History shows that recognizing the dimensions of the problem is the first step in reaching a solution. Susan Aaronson, the seminars' organizer, summed up the issue best by pointing out that so-called free trade agreements exist to, in fact, "regulate" trade, not to free it.

This is an important observation. In reality, almost no one believes in free trade because that would mean no controls on goods, services, capital, or labor. Imagine no border restrictions whatsoever: no visas, passports, or green cards, no screening for agricultural pests and diseases, no excluded contraband, no health restrictions.

Yet the answer to Washington's conundrum is not easily reached. The temptation is to stray into debates about meaningless side issues. In the 1980s, for example, Washington and Tokyo were preoccupied with a debate on whether there should be "managed trade." At the time, managed trade meant that nations such as Japan, which had agreed to lower tariffs and quotas on U.S. goods, should be expected to actually buy U.S. exports. The debate raged for years until it became obvious that despite lowering its tariffs, Japan still was not buying many U.S. exports. The Japanese government continued to maintain huge nontariff barriers in the form of extensive regulations, lax antitrust enforcement, tolerance for domestic cartels, import substitution guidelines, and a policy of directing scarce resources to favored industries. With the help of legions of Washington lobbyists, Tokyo managed to keep the debate in Congress focused on the issue of whether it was unfair for the United States to insist on sales— "ringing cash registers"—of goods such as U.S. semiconductors that, after all, dominated markets in the rest of the world.

SEMINAR TOPICS

Likewise, the question of whether trade agreements should be about anything other than trade has a logical answer: trade already affects many aspects of life, so trade agreements among nations should take this into account. This theme ran throughout NPA's series of six seminars. During the first seminar, Columbia University economist Jagdish Bhagwati, famous for his free market views, allowed that currency controls might be a good idea for developing nations whose economies are particularly susceptible to "here-today, gone-tomorrow" investors and currency traders. He also expressed a refreshing lack of sympathy for U.S. investors who put money into a corrupt country such as Nigeria and then expected the U.S. government to make them whole after their funds were stolen. Trade, Bhagwati seemed to be saying, has consequences beyond the simple decision by two parties to swap one thing for another. However, he was not ready for the United States to dictate minimum wages for workers in India and other poor nations.

The second seminar found the participants agreeing that the Internet could be used more effectively to inform the public about trade, but disagreeing on how much information should be made public and when. Nevertheless, no one suggested that the public should not be part of the debate or that the executive branch could function most effectively by negotiating trade agreements in complete secrecy and then presenting the finished product to Congress for a pro forma rubber stamping.

In the third seminar, the question was, essentially, "Should the government reorganize to do a better job at negotiating trade agreements?" The consensus answer quite properly was, "No, the organization isn't the problem; the content of trade deals is the problem." I.M. Destler, a trade economist at the University of Maryland, recommended that more members of Congress get involved in deciding trade policies, an idea repeated by other panelists. While no one wanted to see the tiny, elite U.S. Trade Representative's office made more bureaucratic, they wanted the process to be more democratic and inclusive.

We got to the heart of the matter at seminar four, which examined how the executive and legislative branches should share responsibility for trade policy. After the infamous Smoot-Hawley Tariff Act of 1930, Congress subsequently limited its lead role in trade policymaking. However, fast track, which gave trade negotiating authority to the executive branch, ran out in 1994, thereby inadvertently restoring congressional power to regulate trade and, coincidentally, to amend trade agreements made by the administration with other nations. Congress is currently debating whether to renew fast track (trade promotion authority).

The seminar's consensus was that granting the executive branch negotiating authority is valuable not because it takes Congress out of the nuts and bolts of the process, but because it is Congress's way of passing along instructions to the executive branch on supposedly tangential items such as labor rights and environmental protections. Congress is now profoundly interested in trade policy. The House/Senate conference committee on the 1974 trade bill included just 14 members from both bodies. With the 1988 trade bill, the number of conferees was up to 200, more than one-third of all Congress.

The fifth seminar included two former trade officials, who admitted that the formal advisory process has not worked as well as Congress intended. Phyllis Bonanno, who ran the private sector liaison office at USTR for 10 years and directed various presidential advisory committees on trade policy, said "If people don't understand the benefits of trade, they really can't give advice." Trade professionals are already sold on the benefits of trade. They just want advice on how to negotiate the best deals on behalf of affected businesses, whom they see as their principal constituency. On the other side, Mark Ritchie, an environmental and agricultural activist, urged the seminar participants to "let go of your ideology and open your minds" to the broader implications of trade. That seemed unlikely.

At the last seminar, Jake Caldwell of the National Wildlife Federation noted that "Trade is not an end in itself. It is a tool to achieve human aspirations, to improve standards of living, and to enhance the quality of life. If it fails to better people's lives," he asked, "then what good is it?" William Lane, Caterpillar's Washington lobbyist, agreed that trade needs to improve lives. It does so, in part, though a largely unappreciated method, he insisted: by supplying Americans with a wider range of goods and services, at a lower cost, than if U.S. borders were closed to imports. Trade agreements, according to Lane, keep the process fluid and fair. Aaronson said we may be getting away from that purpose and assigning too many responsibilities to trade agreements, from protecting endangered species to saving the lives of AIDS sufferers in South Africa.

Whether trade agreements are used as an active tool or whether trade agreements reflect an assortment of society's values, they are certain to grow more complicated. The increasingly democratic and contentious process of arriving at trade policy, as that crowded hearing room showed, is here to stay.

National Policy Association

The National Policy Association was founded in 1934 by distinguished business and labor leaders who believed that the private sector should actively participate in the formulation of public policy. NPA's goal is to seek common ground on effective and innovative strategies that address a range of issues vital to the prosperity of America.

NPA is one of the nation's principal nonpartisan, nonprofit organizations promoting informed dialogue and independent research on major economic and social problems facing the United States. NPA brings together influential business, labor, agricultural, and academic leaders to identify solutions to these emerging challenges. Through its policy committees, NPA provides a broad-based arena where members hear differing viewpoints and gain new insights on issues of mutual concern and national importance. The policy groups include the Committee on New American Realities, the Food and Agriculture Committee, and the North American Committee.

NPA-sponsored research addresses fundamental questions related to strengthening U.S. competitiveness and productivity in a context of justice, equity, and basic human values. Through its research and other projects, NPA seeks to develop pragmatic solutions to the structural and technological changes impacting an increasingly interdependent world. Topical publications, seminars, and conferences help disseminate the conclusions and recommendations of NPA's work.

National Policy Association
1424 16th Street, N.W., Suite 700
Washington, D.C. 20036-2229
Tel (202) 265-7685   Fax (202) 797-5516
npa@npa1.org   www.npa1.org

64

Selected Publications

Taking Trade to the Streets: The Lost History of Public Efforts to Shape Globalization, by Susan A. Aaronson. Available from University of Michigan Press (256 pp, 2001, $29.95).

Trade and the American Dream: A Social History of Postwar Trade Policy, by Susan A. Aaronson. Available from University Press of Kentucky (262 pp, 1996, $18.95).

Trade Is Everybody's Business, by Susan A. Aaronson. Available from the Close Up Foundation (63 pp, 1996, $5.95).

Agricultural Trade Negotiations and the Developing Countries after Seattle, by Mark R. Drabenstott, Richard L. Bernal, Nabil Fahmy, and Bruce Gosper (32 pp, 2001, $10.00), NPA #300.

Income, Socioeconomic Status, and Health: Exploring the Relationships, ed. James A. Auerbach and Barbara Kivimae Krimgold (NPA/Academy for Health Services Research and Health Policy, 2000), NPA #299.

Improving Health: It Doesn't Take a Revolution, ed. James A. Auerbach, Barbara Kivimae Krimgold, and Bonnie Lefkowitz (NPA/Academy for Health Services Research and Health Policy, 2000, $10.00), NPA #298.

New Directions: African Americans in a Diversifying Nation, ed. James S. Jackson (308 pp, 2000, $24.95), NPA #297.

China's WTO Accession: America's Choice, by Richard W. Fisher (16 pp, 2000, $8.00), NPA #296.

The Challenges of Globalization for U.S. Development Assistance, by Emmy Simmons (16 pp, 1999, $5.00), NPA #294.

Creating an International Development Framework, by James D. Wolfensohn (20 pp, 1999, $8.00), NPA #293.

Employment Practices and Business Strategy, ed. Peter Cappelli. Commissioned by the Committee on New American Realities (NAR), available from Oxford University Press and from NPA (240 pp, 1999, $29.95).

NPA is a nonprofit organization under section 501(c)(3) of the Internal Revenue Code.

To order NPA publications and to find out about NPA's Membership Program, visit NPA's Web site, www.npa1.org or contact:

National Policy Association
1424 16th Street, N.W., Suite 700
Washington, D.C. 20036-2229
Tel (202) 265-7685   Fax (202) 797-5516
npa@npa1.org